Aṣṭakāla Līlā Padāvalī

Kavī Rāya Śekhara

Translated by Advaita dāsa

Other Publications

Food for Peace
Prema Vivarta
Ekadasi Mahātmya
The Bhakti Trilogy
Sri Siksastaka
Sri Manah Siksa
Sri Harinama Cintamani
Sri Dana Keli Cintamani
Mukta Caritra
Sri Govinda Lilamrta
Krishna Bhavanamrta Mahavakya
The Glories of Advaita Acarya

Childrens Coloring Books

Gauracandra Part 1&2
Govinda
Gokula
Ayodya

Copyright © 2000 by Rasbihari Lal & Sons
ISBN - 81-87812-04-4

Designed and Layout by Śrī Nitāi dāsa

Published by Rasbihari Lal & Sons
Loi Bazar, Vrindavan-281121 U.P INDIA
Phone: 0565-442570
Fax: 0565-443092
Our other division is Brijwasi Exports

Printed at:
Rakmo Press Pvt. Ltd., New Delhi-110 020.

Kavi Rāya Śekhara was born in the dynasty of Lord Śrī Nityānanda in the district of Vardhamāna. He was a disciple of Śrī Raghunandana Gosvāmī. He was the best writer of Vrajabuli-poetry.

Aṣṭakāla Līlā Padāvalī

🪷

niśānta līlā — kuñja bhaṅga: śukotkaāṭhā
rāgiṇī bhairavī — tāla eka tālā

daśa diśa niramala bhelo parakāś;
sakhīgā mane ghana uṭhaye tarās
āmre kokila ḍāke kadambe mayūr;
dāṛimbe bosiyā kīra boloye madhur
drākṣā-ḍāle bosi ḍāke kapota kapoti;
tārāgaṇa sahite lukāyalo tārāpati

"Spotless (Sun) light pervaded the ten directions and the *sakhīs* became greatly alarmed by this. The cuckoos called in the mango-vines and the peacocks in the Kadamba-trees. The parrots sat in the pomegranate trees and called out sweetly. The male and female pigeons called out on the branches of the grapevines and the stars began to conceal themselves along with their lord (the moon)."

kumudinī vadana tejalo madhukara;
kamala niyaṛe āsi milaye satvara
sārī kohe rāi jāgo colo nija ghor;
jāgalo sakala lok nāhi māno ḍor
śekhara śekhare kohe hāsiyā hāsiyā
cora hoiyā sādhu pārā rohilā śutilā

"The honeybees gave up the faces of the lilies and quickly approached the lotus flowers. The female parrot said: "Rāi, wake up and go home! All the people have awoken! Aren't You afraid?' Rāya śekhara then laughed and told Rasika śekhara (Kṛṣṇa): "You remain there reclining like a saint, although You are a (woman-) thief!" (1)

sakhī janotkaāṭhā
rāgiṇī lalita — tāla eka tālā

ālikula jāgalo alikula gāne;
camakita cāhoi cakita nayāne
cañcala cita ati cololi nikuñje;
sukhada śeja tahi su-kusuma puñje
vigalita kuntala vigalita vāse;
heri heri sahacari koru parihāse

"The *ālis* (girlfriends) woke up from the *alis'* (bees) singing, looking around with startled eyes. With restless minds they entered the *nikuñja* where there was a delightful bed of many nice flowers. Their (Rādhā-Kṛṣṇa's) hairs and garments were dishevelled, seeing which the *sakhīs* made jokes."

jāgo jāgo sundarī sundara kān;
daśa diśa niramalo bhelo vihān
kumudinī teji ali kamala hi gelo;
gurujana ati khane bāhira bhelo
hām sab āchiye tuyā mukha cāi;
rahoi nā pāriye ab ghare jāi

'Wake up, wake up, Sundarī Rādhā and Sundara Kṛṣṇa! The ten directions are already illuminated! The bees have given up the lilies and have gone to the lotus flowers, and Your superiors have already come out of their houses! We are all staring at Your faces, but we cannot stay here — we must go home now!"

jāgalo duhu jana roholo vibhor;
nayana nā melai tanu tanu joṛ
sakhīgā toikhone koru anumān;
kapaṭa koṭi koto koroto bhiyān
duhu jana meli uṭhilo ati bhoy pāi;
hāsi hāsi śekhara dvāra khosāi

"Hearing this, Rādhā and Kṛṣṇa woke up. They could not keep Their eyes open and Their bodies were intertwined. The *sakhīs* then thought: They perform so many millions of false dramas. When They wake up They become very frightened." Rāya śekhara laughs and opens the gate. (2)

madana śayotthāna
rāginī vibhāṣa — tāla eka tālā

rajanī śeṣa-por   nāgarī nāgara,
baithalo śejaki māhi
heri sakhi satvara,   mandira bhitora,
hāsi hāsi paiṭhalo tāhi

"At the end of the night, Nāgarī (heroine Rādhā) and Nāgara (hero Kṛṣā) sat on Their bed of love. When Their girlfriends saw this, they quickly entered the love-cottage, giggling."

sahacari meli,   keli kalāvatī,
koru koto rasa parakāśe
rajanika raṅga,   kohite nava nāgarī,
piyā mukha jhāpoli bāse

"Keli Kalāvatī (Rādhā, who is expert in the arts of the love game) then met with Her girlfriends and revealed so much *rasa* (love mellows). Nava Nāgarī (the young heroine Rādhā) told them all about Her nocturnal pastimes, covering Her beloved's face with Her garment."

duhu mukha nirakhi,   harakhi sab sahacarī,
pulakinī roholo vibhori
pīta vasana lei,   nija tanu jhāmpalo,
lāje lājāyali gori

"Looking at Their faces, all the *sakhīs* got goosepimples of ecstatic love. Gori (golden Rādhā) shyly covered Her own body with Kṛṣṇa's yellow garment."

tabe hari nāgari,   kore āgorali,
ḍubalo sukha sindhu mājh
lalitā lalita kori,   duhuṅ veśa khaṇḍita,
sājāoto anupama sāj

"Then Hari took His heroine upon His lap and drowned in an ocean of bliss. Lovely Lalitā then dressed Them in a matchless way, (removing) Their torn up clothes."

duhuṅ rūpe magana,   bhelo sab sakhīgaṇa,
dina rajanī nāhi jāno
aruṇa udoy bhelo,   jaṭilā śabada pāilo,
kavi śekhara guṇa gān

"The *sakhīs* were absorbed in (staring at) Their forms, forgetting whether it was day or night. Thus the sun rose and they heard the name of Jaṭilā, while Kavi śekhara sings Their glories." (3)

kakkhaṭī vitarka

niśācara ghare gelo,   *aruṅa udoya bhelo*
        tārāpati kāṅti malin
kumuda mudita bhelo,   *paduma prakāśalo,*
        paravaśa poṛolo kaṭhin

"All nocturnal creatures had gone home, the morning red had broken and the luster of the moon, the lord of the stars, had become dimmed. The night-lilies had closed their petals, the lotus flowers had begun to blossom, and those who were controlled by others (Rādhā and Her girlfriends) got into trouble."

dekhiyā dohāra rīte,   *vṛndā vikala cite*
        ādeśilā kokila kokili
tārā sabhe gāna kore,   *bhramara jhaṅkāra pūre*
        kekā kekī koroye vikuli

"Seeing how They both behaved, Vṛndā became anxious and ordered the cuckoos and their wives to sing. They all began to sing along with the buzzing bees and the cooing peacocks and peahens."

kakkhaṭī uṭhāya tān,   *ki koroho rādhā kān*
        śeja teji koroho payān
rāire nā dekhi ghare,   *jaṭilā laguḍa kore,*
        bone āsi koroye sandhān

"The old she-monkey Kakkhaṭī then got up and said: "O Rādhā-Kṛṣṇa! What are You doing? Quickly get up from bed and leave! Not seeing Rāi at home, Jaṭilā is coming to the forest to search for Her, wielding a cane!"

kakkhaṭī kapaṭa kothā,   śuni vṛṣabhānu sutā,
*   tarāse taralo bhelo mon*
rādhā kānu sakhī sāthe,   colilā gopata pathe,
*   turite tejalo sei bon*

"When King Vṛṣabhānu's daughter heard Kakkhaṭī's deceiving words Her mind became very anxious and restless. Thus Rādhā, Kṛṣṇa and Their *sakhīs* went down a secret path and quickly left that forest."

khedilo hariṅī jeno,   aichana ramaṅī-gaṅa,
*   cakita nayane ghana cāy*
nāgarī nāgara pāśe,   dāṛāiye śekhara hāse,
*   bhoy nāi sabāre bujhāy*

"The girls resembled deer that were tormented by a hunter and stared all around with startled eyes. Rāya śekhara stands by the side of Nāgarī Rāi and Nāgara Kṛṣṇa and laughs, saying: "Nobody should fear." (4)

❀

prabhāta samaye gṛhāgamana

duhuṅ rūpa lāvaṅi,   manamatha mohinī,
*   nirakhi nayāna bhūli jāy*
rajani janita rati,   viśeṣa ālāpane,
*   alasa roholo duhuṅ gāy*

"Their elegant forms captivate Cupid, and eyes forget everything when they see Them. They discussed the details of Their nocturnal erotic enjoyments and both felt physically exhausted."

> *vithāralo kuntala,   tāhe kumuda dala,*
> *lolahi ānahi bhāti*
> *duhuṅ doṅhā heri mukha, hṛdaye bārhalo sukha,*
> *bhuli roholo doṅhe māti*

"Their extensive dangling locks were filled with lily-petals, that resembled something else. When They looked at Each other's faces the bliss in Their hearts increased, so much so that They forgot everything else."

> *nija nija mandira,   nāgari nāgara,*
> *coloite sakhī anubandha*
> *viraha viṣānale,   duhuṅ tanu jāralo*
> *locane lāgalo dhandha*

"Under the instigation of the *sakhīs* Nāgarī Rāi and Nāgara śyāma went to Their individual homes. Their bodies were wrecked by the poisonous fire of love-in-separation and Their eyes were bewildered."

> *bhītaka cīta,   putali sama duhuṅ jana,*
> *raholi vidāyaka belā*
> *prema payonidhi,   uchali uchali uṭhi,*
> *cetane acetana bhelā*

"Their hearts were filled with fear and They became stunned like puppets as the moment of separation approached. Thus the milk-ocean of love surged and made the cognisant unconscious."

duhuṅ jana cīta,   rīta heri sahacarī,
ghana ghana gaganahi cāy
rajani pohāyalo,   jana sab jāgalo,
se ḍorahi adhika ḍorāy

"After the *sakhīs* saw how the Divine Pair thought and acted they stared deeply at the sky. The night had ended and all the people had woken up. This made them even more scared."

śekhara bujhiyā tava,   kori koto anubhava,
duhuṅ saṅga bhaṅga korāy
nija nija mandire,   sabhe jāi śūtali,
guru jana bheda nā pāy

"Rāya Śekhara then understands it is time to terminate Their nocturnal union. Everyone then went to their individual homes to recline, without their superiors noticing anything." (5)

✿

gṛhāgamana
rāginī suhai — tāla lophā

koto hu dulaha saṅga bhoi gelo vicched;
gara gara antara bāṛhalo khed
jhara jhara locane śaśimukhī roi;
alakhite āolo lakhai nā koi
sahacarīgaṇa meli śeja bichāi;
alase avaśa dhani śutali tāi
antara gara gara śyāmara leho;
sakhīgaṇa satvare colu nija geho
saba jana pūralo nija nija sādh;
koho kavi śekhara rasa mariyād

"How difficult it was for Them to meet, and now They had to separate again! Their hearts were throbbing of surging grief. Tears streamed from the eyes of weeping moon-faced Rāi. They returned home unnoticed, no one saw Them arrive. The maidservants then met and made a bed, where Rādhā lay senseless of fatigue, Her heart throbbing with love for śyāma. The *sakhīs* also cleverly returned to their own homes. Thus everyone had their desires fulfilled. Kavi śekhara says: "Such are the ways of *rasa*." (6)

vicchede vikala bhelo duhuṅka parāṅa;
dara dara antara jharoye nayāna
duhuṅ mone manasija jāgi rahu;
tila vichuraṅa nahe keho kāhu
niśabade śūtalo ninda nāhi bhāy;
viyoga viyādhi vithāralo gāy
duhuṅka dulaho nehā duhuṅ bhāle jān;
duhuṅ jana milane madhyata pāṅca bāṅa
rāya śekhara jāne iha rasa raṅga;
paravaśa prema satata nahe saṅga

"Both Their hearts became upset with feelings of separation and tears streamed out of Their eyes from within Their hearts. Cupid arose within Their minds and They could not forget Each other even slightly. They lay down on Their beds quietly without feeling any sleep, the disease of separation spreading throughout Their bodies. Both knew very well that Their love was hard to attain— Cupid had to mediate between Them to arrange for a meeting. Rāya śekhara knows that these are the ways of *rasa*. Those who are controlled by others are not always able to meet." (7)

Prātaḥ kāla
rāginī suhinī — tāla soma

ninde nindāyali bālā;
niśi vāsara jāgi bhoi gelo durbalā
taṛita latāvali rāmā;
rati-raṅa charame gharame bhelo śyāmā
ālasa ninda bhāra aṅga athira;
samvaraṅa nāhi kore pītama cīra
mana siddhi sādhali rādhā;
āolo alakhite nā poṛolo bādhā
koho kabi śekhara rāy;
dharama sarama nāgi oṛani bhāy

"This sleeping girl, weakened by staying up all night, awakened. This girl, who shines like a row of lightning-vines, perspired during the heated climax of the erotic battle. Thus She became śyāmā (the best of amorous heroines). Her body wobbled out of exhaustion and drowsiness, and in confusion She took along the garments of Her beloved. Rādhā fulfilled Her mind's desires — She managed to return home without any obstacles. Kavi śekhara says: "This outer garment of Hers reveals Her virtue." (8)

samay anudoy, devyāgamana śayotthāna
rāgiāī vibhāṣa — tāla eka tālā lophā

bhagavati devi samaya se jāno;
rāiko mandire koyolo payāni
śutali dekholi ati viparīta;
guru jana vacana nā mānaye bhīta
tapasvinī korolohi koto anumāna;

koro paraśana kori rāi jāgān
camaki uṭhali dhani tharahari kāṁpi;
pīta vasane sabahu tanu jhāṁpi

"Knowing the time had come, Bhagavatī Paurāamāsī came to Rāi's abode. She saw Her reclining in a very contrary manner, not at all afraid of the words of Her superiors. Thus this ascetic (Paurāamāsī) had so many thoughts. She touched Rāi and woke Her up. Dhani got up and began to tremble violently, Her whole body covered by Kṛṣṇa's yellow cloth."

rati viparīta cihna korotohi goi;
rāge bekata tanu abekata hoi
kara-joṛi rāi praṇati kori devī;
āji saphala dina tuyā pada sevi
kāmanī kāhinī koru koto bande;
devati maṅgala dei suchande
koho kobi śekhara śuno sukumārī;
pīta vasana tuhu rākhoho sāmāri

"She concealed the signs of (Kṛṣṇa's) contrary love enjoyment, which is manifest in *rāga* (passion), but is physically unmanifest. With folded hands Rāi offered Her obeisances to Paurāamāsī-devī, saying: "Now My day is successful by serving your lotus feet." Thus She offered so many praises, and Paurāamāsī devī blessed beautiful (*suchande*) Rādhā with auspicious benedictions. Kavi śekhara says: "Hear me, O tender girl! Keep this yellow cloth!" (9)

paurāmāsīr ukti

āju viparīta dhani dekhaluṅ toy;
samujhi nā pāriye saṁśaya moy
tuyā mukha maṇḍala puṅamika cāṅd;
kāhe lāgi bhoi gelo aichana chāṅd
nayana yugala bhelo kājara vithār;
adhara nirasa koru kon gowār
pīna payodhare nakha rekha delo;
kanaka kumbha janu bhagano bhoi gelo
aṅge vilepana heri kuṅkuma bhār;
pītāmbara dhoru ithe ki vicār
sujana ramaṅi tuhuṅ kulavati vād;
kā soye bhuñjali maramaka sādh
kāminī kātara devi samvāde;
koho kavi śekhara boṛo paramāde

"O fortunate girl! Today I see everything upside down! I don't understand and I doubt. Your face resembles the full moon— why does such splendour arise? Eyeliner is smeared all around Your eyes— which impudent boy has parched Your lips like that and has left these scratches on Your big breasts? It almost looks as if these two golden jugs have been broken. I see a lot of *kuṅkuma* smeared over Your body. Why are You wearing this yellow cloth? You have a reputation as a chaste house wife— with whom have You enjoyed this heart's affair?" In great joy the poet Rāya śekhara describes the anxious conversation between the two *devīs* Paurāamāsī and Rādhā. (10)

tuyā aṅge pītima cīre; kuca-yuga daṁśalo kīre
adhara bimba phala tori; ko rasa nelo nicori

vacana bolasi āna bhāti; kā soye vañcali rāti
hṛdoya nayana gati rīta; heroite pāyaluṅ bhīta
iha rasa kāhinī kohoi; jaratī uthi tahi coloi
rāya śekhara anumāne; rāiko amiyā sināne

"I see You have a yellow cloth on Your body and a parrot has bitten Your breasts. Who has stolen the juice from the Bimba-fruits of Your lips? You say one thing but You show another thing. With whom have You spent the night? I get scared when I see the conduct of Your heart and eyes. Tell me this *rasika* narration. When Jaṭilā wakes up I will go. Rāya śekhara thinks: "Rāi is bathing in nectar." (11)

❦

dāsīgāna āyojana
rāgiāī vibhāṣa — tāla eka tālā

niśi avasāne,   saba dāsīgaṇe,
  satvare koroye kāj
veśera mandira ,mājalo sundara,
  rākhalo veśera sāj
  ki nā se dāsīra rīta?
jāniyā marama,   koroye karama,
  jāhāte āpana jit

"At the end of the night all the maidservants quickly got to work, entering into the beautiful dressing room where they kept all the dresses and apparel. Who knows the customs of these maidservants? They serve śrī Rādhikā exactly according to Her wishes, and thus they subdue Her with their service."

daśana mājanī,   rasanā śodhanī,
  thuilo thālite bhori

karpūra sahita,   gandha cūrṅita,
    jatana koriyā dhari

"They placed toothbrushes and tongue-scrapers on trays and carefully held fragrant powder mixed with camphor in their hands."

nirmala salila,   sugandhi śītala,
    pūriyā gāgari jhāri
mukha pākhālite,   sināna korite,
    vedika upore dhari

"They poured spotless cool and fragrant water from pitchers, washed Rādhā's face and seated Her upon a platform to bathe Her."

gāmchā kāciyā,   nirjala koriyā
    rākhalo pṛthak kori
e taila āmalā,   ānalo śyāmalā
    viniyā viniyā bhori

"They squeezed out the towels and thus rid them of the water, before keeping them separately. śyāmalā then brought Amalikā oil and anointed Rādhikā with it."

ubaṭana kori,   kanaka mañjarī,
    ānalo rāiera tore
mañjarī ratana,   koriyā jatana,
    ānalo sināna cīre

"Kanaka Mañjarī brought Rāi's *udvartana* (massaging powder) and Ratna Mañjarī carefully brought Her bathing garments."

guṅavatī tathi,   karpūra mālati,
    sugandhi salila kori

vidhi agocara, nānā upahāra,
thālite thālite bhori

"Young (*karpura mālati*) Guṇavatī brought fragrant water, filling vessels with different paraphernalia that are not perceived even by Lord Brahmā."

vicitra vasana, tāhāte ḍhākana,
korolo parama sukhe
rāiyera iṅgite, rākhalo gopate,
jeno āne nāhi dekhe

"Most blissfully she covered these pots with wonderful sheets (or: She concealed Kṛṣṇa's wonderful cloth). On Rāi's indication she kept them hidden so that no outsiders would see them."

karpūra tāmbūla, mālatira māla,
śekhara jatane kore
se pīta vasana, āniyā tokhona
āpani āoyāse dhare

"Rāya Śekhara carefully brought camphor-laced betelleaves and Mālatī-garlands. Then he brought Kṛṣṇa's yellow cloth personally into his/her abode." (12)

❀

divā arddha daāḍa kāruāya snāna
eka daāḍāvadhi kānta mohana veśa
rāgiāī bhāṭiyāri — tāla eka tālā

pāi avasare, bosilā satvare,
sab sakhīgaṇa mājhe
tabe sakhigaṇa, khosāya bhūṣaṇa,
porāya sināna sāje

"Getting the opportunity, Rādhikā quickly sat down, surrounded by all of Her *sakhīs*. The *sakhīs* then peeled off all of Her ornaments and dressed Her in a bathing gown."

sakhi dekho nā rāiko raṅga!
rati pati koti,   bindhilā yubatī,
ābharaṇe dilo bhaṅga

"Sakhi! Why don't you behold the pastimes of Rāi! How many Cupids have pierced this young girl, breaking Her ornaments?"

hāsa parihāse,   bosiyā āyāse
mukhāni mājalo nīre
mājalo yatane,   daśana rasanā,
śodhalo marīca cure

"Amidst joking and laughter, the *sakhīs* carefully seated Rāi and washed Her face with water. They carefully cleaned Her teeth and tongue and rubbed them with powdered pepper."

toila āmalakī,   dilo saba sakhī,
ubaṭane tuli mālā
sugandhi salile,   sināna koriyā
śītala hoilo bālā

"The *sakhīs* provided oils like āmalakī and applied a virtual garland of *udvartana* powders (a kind of soap powder). Then they bathed Her in fragrant water so that this young girl became cool."

gāmchā āniyā,   gākhāni mochāiyā,
*   porāya nīlima bāsa*
veśera mandire,   bosilā satvare,
*   sakhīgaṅa cāri pāśa*

"The *sakhīs* then brought a towel and dried off Rādhikā's entire body before dressing Her in a blue garment. Quickly they seated Her in Her dressing chamber, where They surrounded Her again."

se kāle vistāra,   ṣoḍaśa śiṁgāra,
*   koriyā heraye mukha*
kṛṣṇa avaśeṣa,   koriyā paraśa,
*   pāilo parama sukha*

"They then adorned Her with the sixteen *śṛṅgāra* ornaments and beheld Her face. Getting the touch of Kṛṣṇa's remnants, śrī Rādhikā attained the topmost bliss."

kohe raṅgalatā,   dhani śuno kothā,
*   tomāre nibāra tore*
kundalatā heno,   dekhinu ekhono
*   pośilo jaṭilā ghore*

"Raṅgalatā said: "Listen, O fortunate girl! I saw Kundalatā entering Jaṭilā's house just now. She's coming to take You (to mother Yaśodā's abode)."

se saba kāhinī,   śuni vinodinī,
*   pulake pūrilo gāy*
rāiyera iṅgite,   vāratā bujhite,
*   cololo śekhara rāy*

"When Rāi Vinodinī heard all this, Her body became studded with goosepimples. Understanding Rai's beckoning, Rāya śekhara then hurries off to see what's going on. (13)

❀

vrajeśvarīr utkāṭhā
rāgiāī suhai — tāla lophā

niśi avasāna jāni nandera gharaṅī;
dās-dāsī ḍākiyā kohoye priya vāṅī
āmāra jīvana dhana kānāi bolāi;
lālibe pālibe tāre tomarā sabāi
jāra jei kāj bāchā koro mon diyā;
āmi ār ki bolibo bujho vicāriyā
rāṅīra udāra bol śuni dāsa dāsī;
āveśe koroye karma premānande bhāsi

"When the night had turned into morning Nanda's wife spoke sweet words to her male and female servants: "Kṛṣṇa and Balarāma are the treasures of my life— take good care of Them, all of you! O boys and girls! Perform your duties attentively! What more can I say? Just consider this properly!" When the servants and maidservants heard Queen Yaśodā's noble words they began to perform their duties, floating in ecstatic love."

kundalatā āni tathā kohe jaśomatī;
rādhāre ānoho bāchā koriyā samhati
śuni paraṅām kori cole kundalatā;
jaṭilāre namaskari nivedaye kothā
dekhi ānandita hoilo jaṭilāra cita;
śekhara colilā tabe pāiyā iṅgita

"Yaśomatī then called for Kundalatā and told her: "Oh my daughter! Bring Rādhā here!" Hearing this, Kundalatā offered her obeisances unto Mother Yaśodā and left. (Coming to Yāvat) She offered her obeisances unto Jaṭilā and told her what Queen Yaśodā had said. Seeing her, Jaṭilā became ecstatic. Rāya śekhara then went there, receiving a hint to do so." (14)

aruāodaye — yāvaṭe kundalatār āgamana
rāginī jaya-jayantī — tāla eka tālā

dekhiyā kundalatā,   jaṭilā unamata,
    parama ānande nācaye
dhariyā kori kole,   titala āṅkhi lore,
    kuśala vāratā puchaye

"Seeing Kundalatā, Jaṭilā began to dance in ecstatic frenzy. Holding Kundalatā to her chest she showered her with her tears and inquired about her welfare."

o mora bāchani,   satya kāhinī,
    kohobi nikaṭahi mohari
to heno kulavati,   jagate nāhi koti
    hāmāri viśoās tohāri

"O my daughter! I tell you something frankly—There are not so many chaste girls in this world like you — I have full faith in you!"

gopa pura bhori,   joto hu sundarī,
    kāhuka nā rohu lāj
to heno pativratā,   nā dekhi jati satī
    ghoṣaye lakhimī samāj

"In this cowherders' settlement there are so many beautiful girls, but none of them have any shame left. I can not find a chaste girl who is dedicated to her husband like you anywhere anymore. This is proclaimed within the society of goddesses of fortune!"

haraṣi kundalatā,   bharasi kohe kothā,
* kotohu binoy vibhārasi*
catura śekhara,   jarati antara,
* kotoye jatane sudhāyasi*

"Blissfully Kundalatā spoke so many humble and anxious words. Clever Rāya śekhara carefully scans the heart of Jaṭilā." (15)

❀

divā arddha daāḍe — yuvati paricaryā
rāginī dhānaśī — tāla eka tāla

se je vrajeśvarī,   nā jāne cāturī,
* parama udāra seho*
jokhon jā bole,   tokhoni tā bhūle
* sabāre samāna leho*

"This Queen of Vraja is not a trickster— she is most generous. Whatever anyone says she forgets it instantly. She loves everyone equally."

hede go ārijā mā!
se jana āmāre,   pāṭhāilā satvare
* dekhite tomāra pā*

"O revered mother, hear me! This person has sent me here quickly to see Your lotus feet!"

> *cūna khoṛa dhori,*   *daśana upori,*
>   *je sab kohilo rānī*
> *se soba śunite,*   *heno loya cite,*
>   *pāṣāna goloye jāni*

"I'm wearing dust and straw on the teeth (I totally submit myself) to whatever the Queen says. Hearing it causes even stones to melt, I have taken it to heart."

> *māsīra caraṅe,*   *kohiyā vacane,*
>   *gopate ānibe bahu*
> *alakhite pathe,*   *āsibā turite,*
>   *jemate nā dekhe kehu*

"She submits the request to Māsī (maternal aunt)'s Jaṭilā's feet to secretly bring her daughter-in-law. Quickly bring Her over a secret path, so that no one will see Her!"

> *śuniyā minati,*   *ulasi jarati,*
>   *colilā rāiyera ghare*
> *kundalatā kore,*   *sompiyā vadhūre*
>   *rānīre āśīṣa kore*

"Hearing this humble request Jaṭilā happily went to Rāi's room. Placing her daughter-in-law in Kundalatā's hands she blessed Her."

> *rāi koro loiyā,*   *nija śire diyā,*
>   *kohoye kātara bol*
> *kulera dharama,*   *putrera sarama,*
>   *sakala rākhobi mora*

"Taking Rāi's hand and placing it on her own head Jaṭilā anxiously said: "Protect the virtue of our family and the welfare of my son.""

jaśodā tanaya, nā māne binoya,
 tāhāre āmāra ḍora
nibhṛte ketane, āsibe jatane,
 jāhāte nā hāse pora

"The son of Yaśoda has no respect for anything or anyone. It is Him who I fear. Try carefully to approach their home in secret, so that no one will ridicule us."

kundalatā kohe, tumi devī mohe,
 caraṇa paraśi tor
śekharera ṭhāi, kono ḍor nāi,
 sevane bhorasā mora

"Kundalatā said: "You are my goddess, I touch your feet. When you are with Rāya Śekhara you need not fear. Devotional service is my great aspiration." (16)

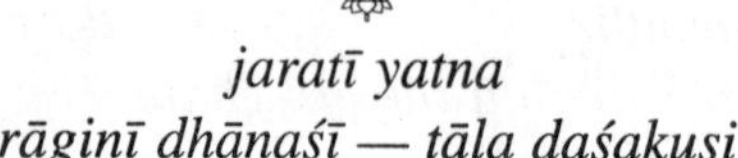

jaratī yatna
rāginī dhānaśī — tāla daśakusi

jaratī jatana kori, kohe śuno sundarī
 sakhī saṅge koroho payāṅ
uṛaṅī ghoṛaṅi māthe, dekhiyā colibe pathe,
 lakhite nā pāre jeno ān

"Jaṭilā diligently told Rāi: "Hear me, O Sundari! Go now with Your sakhīs! Cover Your head with Your veil while You're on the way, so that no one can notice You!"

baṛora jhiyāri baṭa, kule śīle naha choṭa,
 sab guṇe hao paravīna
thākiho sabāra mājhe, bujhibā āpana kāje
 āmi ār jībo koto dina?

"You are the daughter of a great chieftain and Your family and reputation are not slight. Indeed You are greatly qualified! Stay in the middle of Your group of *sakhīs* and understand Your duty. Who knows how many days I have left to live?"

sadaye vidāya kore,   jaṭilā colilā ghare,
ulasita rasavatī rādhe
raṅginī saṅginī tāra,   loi sab upahāra,
cololi pūrāite sādhe

"After pitifully granting leave to Rādhikā, Jaṭilā went back inside her home. Meanwhile Rasavatī Rāi set out in great joy with Her playful girlfriends, taking all their paraphernalia along for the satisfaction of their desires."

gajendra gamana jini,   cole rāi vinodinī,
sughaḍa sakhīra heli aṅga
kohoye śekhara rāy,   puchite puchite jāy,
rajanī vilāsa rasa raṅga

"Thus Rāi Vinodini (delightful Rādhā) walked with a gait defeating that of the king of elephants, leaning Her body against Her loving girlfriends. Rāya śekhara says: "They asked Her about Her *rasika* pastimes of the previous night." (17)

rasodgāra: sakhī vitarka
rāgiāī paṭha mañjarī — eka tālā

e dhani aichana kohobi moy; āju je koichana dekhiye toy
nayāna bayān ānahi bhāti; kohite kāhinī bhulasi pāti

suraṅga adhara viraṅga bheli; kā soye kāminī koyoli keli
bekata bhoi gelo gopata kāj; ataye kāhāre koroho lāj
saghane jaghana kāṁpaye tor; madana mathana koyolo jor

"O fortunate girl, tell me one thing—how am I seeing you today? Your face and eyes look different today.
When you tell me this story you forget your whereabouts.
Your otherwise colorful lips have lost their colour. Who is
it that this girl has played with? As Your secret activities
have become public, for whom should You be ashamed?
You are shivering profusely, Cupid must have shaken You
up violently."

gaura payodhara bhelo hu rāt; nakhera ācara jhāpasi tāt
khinahu khinahu heriye tāi; saghane vadane uṭhiche hāi
pulake pūrita sakala gā; colite nā cole athira pā
amiyā sāgara tuhu se rāi; mukunda mātaṅga bihare tāi
te bujhiye mana vitathā dekhi; bekata koriyā nā koho sakhi
kohoye śekhara ki koro lāje; koho ṇā kāhinī sakhira mājhe

"You are concealing red nail-marks on Your golden
breasts with Your cloth. I see You're getting more and
more emaciated (or distressed), and Your face issues a loud
yawn. Your whole body is studded with goosepimples but
You cannot move with such unsteady feet. O Rāi! You are
an ocean of nectar wherein the Mukunda-elephant sports.
Understanding this to be mental delusions, don't reveal
this, O *sakhi*, don't speak anymore. Rāya śekhara says:
"Whence the shame? Tell these tales amongst the *sakhīs*!"
(18)

rasodgāra
śrī rāga — yati

ki kohobo re sakhi tohāri samāja;
kohoite kāhini lāgaye lāj
śūti ghumāyaluṅ hām ageyāna;
alakhite āolo nāgara kān
pīna payodhare delahi hāta;
turite lukāyaluṅ deha vigāta
taba hi adhara rasa pībaye mor;
jāgalo manamatha bāndhaluṅ cor
thara thara kāmpaye kore āgori; t
aba hām chuṭaluṅ ninda vibhori
korobo kopa jāni choilo se kāna;
joi koholo mohe koi se jāna
parirambhaṅa beri mṛdaluṅ āṅkhi;
tāhe je bhoi gelo śekhara sākhi

"O *sakhi,* what can I say to you? It is embarrassing to tell you what happened. I lay down and fell asleep and while I was in ignorance Nāgara Kāna approached Me unnoticed. He placed His hands on My big breasts and I quickly hid them. Then He continued to drink the juice from My lips, which caused Cupid to arise and bind up this thief. His whole body began to tremble and that broke My slumber. Knowing that I would be angry with Him, Kṛṣṇa ran off. Who knows what He has said to Me? Rāya śekhara, though, is a witness to what has happened when He embraced You when Your eyes were closed." (19)

dhānaśī — tāla lophā

hām abalā nārī kiye guṅa jāna;
so rasamaya tanu rasika sujāna

koto hu jatane more kore bosāi;
bāndhalo veṅī se kavarī khosāi
kañcuka deyolo hiyā pora mora;
paraśi payodhara bhoi gelo bhor
kaṇṭhe porāyalo maṅimaya hār;
aṅge vilepana kuṅkuma bhār
vasana porāyalo kori koto chanda;
kiṅkiṅī jālahi koru nīvi bandha
nija kara pallave majhu mukha mājh;
sājāolo nayana kājala āṅj
alakā tilaka dei camaki nehāri;
koho kavi śekhara jāo bolihāri

"I am a weak woman! What do I know about His glories? This *rasika sujāna* (great relisher) has a succulent body. How carefully He seated Me on His lap and bound My braid when it loosened! He replaced My blouse and when He thus touched My breasts I became completely overwhelmed! He hung a jewel necklace around My neck and anointed My body with a lot of vermilion. He dressed Me so expertly, locking a belt of bells and tying a girdle around My waist. With His own lotus-hands He touched My face and placed nice collyrium around My eyes. He marked *tilaka* on My forehead and beheld it in astonishment. Kavi śekhara says: "Bravo, bravo!" (20)

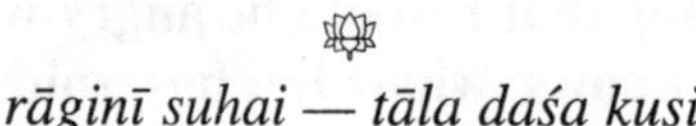

rāgiṇī suhai — tāla daśa kusi

ciruṅi kore dhari,   *keśa veśa kori,*
  sinthete dei sindūra
lāsa veśa kori,   *vasana porāyai,*
  pāye dhari porāye nūpura

"He took a comb in His hand and combed My hair. Then He dressed Me in *vilāsa veśa* (dress suitable for enjoyment) and placed *sindūra* in My part. After replacing My garments He hung anklebells on My feet."

soi! piyā guṇa kohone nā jāy
dārida hema jeno,   tileka nā choḍai
rabhaye rajani gowāy

"*Sakhi*! My beloved's attributes are indescribable! He did not leave Me for even a moment, just as a poor man never leaves gold. Thus We spent the night enjoying."

so mora śrama jala,   āñcare mochai,
dei vasanaka vāy
campaka māla janu,   samāna sāje tanu,
hiyā vinu śeje nā śoyāy

"He used a cloth to wipe the perspiration from My body and fanned Me with a garment. He decorated My body like a Campaka-garland, He would not lay Me on the bed without a heart."

cibuka dhari mukha,   saghane nehārai,
je kichu kohoye mañjulā
adhara nīrasa,   heriyā cumboi,
ādare khāoyāy tāmbūla

"He held My chin and stared at My face and whatever He said was so lovely! Seeing that My lips were parched He kissed them and affectionately fed Me a *pān*."

rabhasa ālase,   nayana mudi rohu,
camaki saghane jāgāy

kānuka piṭha dei,   kobohu nā śūtiye,
sakhi ghume āṅkhi ḍhulāy

"My eyes remained closed out of *rasika* fatigue but still I stayed awake in astonishment; I could never recline with My back towards Kṛṣṇa. O *sakhi*! My eyes were filled with sleep."

vṛndāvana bhori,   rasera bādara,
dina rajanī nāhi jāno
kṛpaṇa dhana sama,   tileka nā choṛai,
kavi śekhara paramāṇa

"Thus all of Vṛndāvana was filled with a shower of *rasa*, so that night could not be distinguished from day. Just as a miser never parts with his money (so They can never part with Each other). Take Kavi śekhara's word on it." (21)

✿

atha prabhāta samaye nandīśvare
alakṣite śrī kṛṣāer āgaman o śayan

rasavatī saṅge, jāgi rasa raṅge;
aruṇima raṅge, nayana vibhaṅge
madana taraṅge, taralita aṅge;
vasana vibhaṅge, pahirali raṅge
āyalo niśaṅke, śutalo pālaṅke;
kehu nāhi sandhe, rādhe anubandhe
madana vibhaṅge, jubati kalaṅke;
kiye bhelo śobhā, śekhara lobhā

"Kṛṣṇa's eyes had become red and restless due to staying up all night, performing joyful *rasika* pastimes

with Rasavatī Rāi. His body billowed on Cupid's waves, and He wore His garments topsy-turvy due to all the joyful pastimes They had performed. Fearlessly He returned home and reclined on His bed without anyone noticing it. Rādhā managed the same feat. This young girl was disgraced in Cupid's play. How beautiful it was, attracting Rāy śekhara!" (22)

yaśodā kartṛk śrī kṛṣāer jāgaraā

> *sabhāre sakala,   kāje niyojiyā,*
> *ānande nandera rāṅī*
> *kānura śayana,   bhavane āsiyā,*
> *kohoye madhura vāṅī*

"Blissfully Nanda's Queen engaged everyone in their duties. Coming into Kṛṣṇa's bedroom, she spoke sweet words."

> *uṭhoho bāchani,   mu jāw nichani,*
> *ālasa koroho dūr*
> *āsiyā chāowāl,   āṅginā bhorolo,*
> *udoya korilo sūr*

"O my child, wake up! Please cast aside Your fatigue now! The courtyard is filled with cowherd boys and the sun has risen!"

> *rāmera vasana,   porilā kokhoṇo,*
> *ke nilo vasana tor*
> *rātā utapala,   nayana yugala,*
> *ki lāgi dekhiye bhor*

"Since when are You wearing Balarāma's cloth? Who has taken Your cloth? Why do I see Your eyes being red, despite the fact that it is morning (and You are supposed to have slept tightly throughout the night)?"

nīla nalina,   ātape malina,
*   keno vā emona deho*
unamata hoiyā,   bulaho dhāiyā,
*   ku diṭhi dile vā keho*

"Why does Your body resemble a blue lotus flower that is withered by the sun? Is it because You have been running around like mad or because someone cast an evil spell on You?"

hiyāra upora,   kaṅṭaka āṅcaṛa
*   giyāchilā kon bone?*
āmāra kapāle,   nā jāni ki phole,
*   parāṅe moribo mene*

"Have You perhaps entered some thorny bushes that have scratched Your chest? Who knows what *karma* I have to suffer that I must die like this (of anxiety)?"

devatā koteko,   dānava joteko,
*   phiraye gahana bone*
se sob dekhilo,   tāhā je hoilo,
*   henoi bāsoi mane*

"I suppose all this can also have happened because of all the gods and demons that ramble through the forests."

devera kāroṅe,   maṅgalācaraṅe,
*   pūjibo sināna kori*

e dadhi odana,   brāhmaṅe jatane,
  bhuñjābo udora bhori

"I will bathe and perform auspicious worship of the Lord (for Your protection) and I will carefully feed rice and yoghurt to the *brāhmaāas*, thus filling up their bellies."

māyera vacane.   jāgiyā tokhone,
  hāsaye gokula rāy
devatā sevinī,   āilā tokhoni,
  jaśodā bandilo pāy

"When Gokula Rāy (Kṛṣṇa) heard these words from His mother, He smiled and got up. The pious goddess Paurāamāsī then appeared and Yaśodā offered her obeisances unto her feet."

rāṅira nandana,   gaurīra caraṅa,
  saghane japana kore
śekhara yugati,   śuno yaśomati,
  ki bhoy tāhāre tore

"Rāy Śekhara counsels mother Yaśodā, saying: "Listen, O Yaśomati! Why should you be afraid of anything? Your son is always absorbed in *japa* (worship) of Gaurī's (Rādhā's) lotus feet!" (23)

❁

śrī kṛṣāer śayotthāna mukha prakṣālana o go dohana
  rāginī dhānaśī — tāla rūpaka

devatī āsiyā, gharete pośiyā, śayane dekhiyā kān
gāye hāt diyā, tāre jāgāiyā, korāilo sābadhāna
satvare uṭhiyā, tāhāre vandiyā, nayāna kacāle hāte
āśīṣa pāiyā, bāhira hoiyā, mililā sakhāra sāthe

35

joto dāsagaṅa,   koriyā jatana, dhoyāilo mukha cāṅde
 dekhiyā vadana, moroye madana, phāṅpare poriyā kānde
sakhāgaṅa saṅge,   nānā rasa raṅge,   kharike āilo hari
gābhī vatsa sab,   kore hamvārab ,dohaye muṭaki bhori
dohana mohana,   nā jāy kathana,   ānande ākula gāi
śekhara jatane,   kohoye gopane,   e pathe āsibe rāi

"Bhagavatī Paurāamāsī came and sat down in Kṛṣṇa room to watch Him reclining. Then she woke Him up and warned Him (not to spill the beans) by stroking His body with her hand. Kṛṣṇa quickly got up and offered His obeisances unto her, rubbing His eyes with His hands. Receiving her blessings He went outside and met all His chums. All His servants then gathered to carefully rinse His moon-like face. Seeing Kṛṣṇa's face, even Cupid was struck and began to weep of embarrassment. Hari then came to the meadows, playing different *rasika* pastimes with His friends. The cows and calves began to bellow and the milk pots brimmed over with milk. The cow-milking of Mohana is indescribable and agitates the cows with ecstasy. Rāya śekhara carefully and secretly says: "Rāi will come over this path." (24)

❀

rādhā-kṛṣāer rūpāvalambana milana
rāgiāī vibhāṣa — tāla eka tālā

rajanī kāhinī,   kohite ramaṅī,
          pulake pūralo dehā
anaka varaṅī,   ki hoilo nā jāni,
          soṅri se sab lehā

"As this fair lady related Her nocturnal pastimes She got goosepimples all over Her body. Who knows what

happened with this golden girl as She remembered Her loving pastimes?"

> *angera vasana,   khasaye saghana,*
>   *nayane bhoroye lora*
> *viṣāde vikala,   visori sakala*
>   *caraṅa nā cole thora*

"Her garments fell off Her body and tears streamed from Her eyes. Agitated by sorrow She forgot everything (external) and Her feet did not tread even slightly anymore."

> *hṛdaya mandire,   pirīti pālaṅke,*
>   *rasera bāliśa tāy*
> *ārati toṣali,   tāhāte pātali,*
>   *śutalo rasika rāy*

"In the temple of Her heart there is a bed of love and on this bed is a pillow of relish. There She spread out a *toṣaka* (small mattress) and laid Her Rasika Rāy (Kṛṣṇa, the king of relishers) to rest on it."

> *piyāra pirīti,   kohoye yuvatī,*
>   *dhariyā sakhira kore*
> *ekhara satvare,   kohoye rādhāre*
>   *dekhibe nāgara vare*

"This young girl spoke of Her beloved's love, while holding Her girlfriend's hand. Rāya Śekhara then swiftly tells Rādhā: 'You will see Your lover (again).'" (25)

nāgara unmatta māyūra

rādhā mukha śaśi,   heraite ākula,
bhoi gelo nanda kiśora
nija kula dharama,   karama sab vichuralo
vichuralo chāndana ḍora

"When Nanda's son saw Rādhā's moon-like face He became greatly agitated, forgetting His family tradition, His duties and His rope for tying up the calves."

hari hari iha kiye bhelo hi raṅga
vichuralo kānu śṛṅga vetra veṅu,
vichuralo agraja saṅga

"Hari Hari! What ecstasy! Kṛṣṇa forgot His horn, reed and flute and His elder brother's presence!"

vichuralo śrīdāma subala madhumaṅgala
vichuralo yuddhaka ṣaṅḍa
mana māhā madana mahodadhi uchalalo
vichuralo dohana bhāṅḍa

"He forgot (the presence of) śrīdāma, Subala and Madhumaṅgala, and He forgot about His fighting bulls. Cupid was surging in His mind in such a way that He forgot about His milk-bucket!"

heraite bhāvini so rūpa lāvaṅi;
tanu mana koro anubandhe
khaḍika samīpa sudhāmukhi mīlalo;
rāy śekhara poṛu dhande

"When He beheld the elegant form of Bhāvinī Rāi His mind and body sought Her. Close to the meadows He met nectar-faced Rādhā, and Rāya śekhara becomes bewildered (by the sight). (26)

rāginī bhūpālī — tāla lophā

patha gati nayane milalo rādhā kāna;
duhuṅ mane manaśija pūralo sandhāna
duhuṅ mukha heraite duhu bhelo bhor;
samaya nā bujhato acatura cor
vidagadha saṅginī sab rasa jān;
kuṭila nayane koyolo sābdhān
colilā rājapathe duhu avaṣāi;
koho kavi śekhara duhu caturāi

"On the way, Rādhā and Kṛṣṇa's eyes met and Their minds were thus grateful targets for Cupid. They both became absorbed in staring at Each other's faces, and became so captivated that They lost notion of time and circumstances. The clever *sakhīs* understood Their feelings and warned Them with crooked glances. Thus They moved over the royal road and Kavi śekhara speaks of Their cleverness." (27)

śrī rāga — tāla doṭhuki

rāire dekhiyā,　　　　*umati hoiyā,*
　　　jaśodā korolo kore
mukhāni dhariyā,　　　*cumbana korite,*
　　　bhāsalo nayana lore

"Seeing Rāi, Yaśodā went mad (with love) and took Her on her lap. Holding Her face, she kissed it while floating in her own tears."

> se je rasavatī,   korolo praṇati,
>   jaśodā rohiṇī pāy
> priya sakhīgaṇa,   gopata vasana,-
>   sompolo dhaniṣṭhā ṭhāy

"This *rasavatī* (good cook, humorous girl, or good lover) offered Her obeisances unto the feet of Yaśodā and Rohiāī. Her *priya sakhīs* meanwhile secretly returned Kṛṣṇa's cloth to Dhaniṣṭhā."

> pāiyā vasana,   korolo gopana,
>   dhaniṣṭhā jatanakori
> koriyā ādara,   loi upahāra,
>   rāṇīra nikaṭe dhori

"Receiving the cloth, Dhaniṣṭhā carefully concealed it. Carefully she took some gifts and held them close to Queen Yaśodā."

> vividha vidhāna,   dekhiyā pakkānna,
>   hariṣa tāhāra cita
> jaśodā rohiṇī,   bujhalo kāhinī,
>   dekhiyā rāira rīta

"Seeing the different arrangements that had been made to cook foodstuffs, her heart became very joyful. Yaśodā and Rohiāī, who understood what had happened, observed Rāi's manners."

> āsi dāsīgaṇa,   rādhāra caraṇa,
>   dhoyāilo śītala nīre

ati sukomala,   o thala kamala,
*   mochalo pātala cīre*

"Rāi's maidservants then appeared, washed Her lotus feet with cold water, and wiped these very tender land lotuses (feet) dry with thin towels."

rohiṅī sahite,   randhana korite,
*   bosilo rājāra jhi*
sab sakhīgaṅa,   yogāya yogāna,
*   śekhara yogāya ghi*

"Then this princess sat down with Rohiāī to cook. All the *sakhīs* handed Her the ingredients and Rāy śekhara hands Her the *ghī* (clarified butter)." (28)

❀

śrī rāga — tāla eka tālā

niśi avasāne,   dāsa dāsī gaṅe,
*   tvarāy koroye kāje*
jār jei kāma,   kore anupāma,
*   sabāi sabhāre tāje*

"At the end of night the servants and maidservants quickly got up to perform their duties. They all performed their duties incomparably, everyone enthusing everyone else."

deva purandara,   jini tāra ghara,
*   randhana mandira sāje*
dhaniṣṭhā sundarī,   randhana sāmagrī
*   dharolo tāhāra mājhe*

"Beautiful Dhaniṣṭhā brought all the ingredients for cooking into the kitchen of the abode (of Nanda Mahārāja) which defies the palace of Indra, the king of the demigods."

jvālite indhana,   *ānalo candana,*
deolo jatana kori
bosite āsana,   *jalera bhājana,*
tāhāra nikaṭe dhori

"She brought sandal for firewood and carefully sat down on an *āsana,* keeping a waterpot close to herself."

suśīlā sundarī,   *rasera cāturī,*
vividha randhāna jāne
vidhi agocara,   *nānā upahāra,*
korolo āpana mane

"Beautiful and well-mannered Rādhikā is very expert in cooking and She knows how to make different delicacies. According to her own fancy She made different preparations, that are not perceived even by Lord Brahma."

karpūra mālatī,   *korolo jubatī,*
mano lobhā manoharā
koyolo kadamā,   *reuṛi padumā*
mati cura sumadhurā

"This young girl made delicious Manoharā *laḍḍus* with camphor and nutmeg (*mālatī-phala*), Kadamā (a round and hard sweetmeat shaped like a Kadamba-flower), rhubarb, Padmā-cini-sweets, and very sweet Maticura (small globular sweets)."

amṛta kelikā,   vividha laḍḍukā,
        cāki-khaṅḍa padma cini
gajā khājā peṛā,   cānā candracūṛā,
        michiri māriyā pheni

(She also made) Amṛta Keli-pies, different *laḍḍus*, Cāki-khaāḍa (round balls of rock candy), Padma Cini (lotus-sugar), Gajā (sweets made of flour), Khājā (sweets made with sugar and flour), Peṛā (milk sweets), Cānā (chick-pea fried crisps), Candracūṛā (lit: moonlight), Michiri (Miśrī, or rock candy), Māriyā and Pheāi."

luci puri kori,   rasa pāka bhari,
        sarabhājā sara puri
buṅdi rasa-karā,   rasapura jhurā,
        jatana koriyā kori

"She carefully made Lucis (small *puris*), Puris, succulent Sarabhājā (sweets prepared by frying milk-film), Sarapuri, Bundi (small round sweets of chickpea-powder, dipped in sugar-water), Rasa-karā (a sweet and juicy drop made of the kernel of coconut) and granular dry Rasapura."

sugandhi śītala,   koriyā nirmala,
        bhoriyā sonāra thāli
bhojana bhavane,   rākhilo jatane,
        ḍhākiyā netera phāli

"She filled golden trays with all these fragrant, cool and spotless preparations and carefully kept them in the dining room, covering them with thin sheets."

rasālā mathani,   korolo ramanī,
        khaṅḍa maṅḍa ādi joto

lachimī ketane,   nāhiko jatane,
  nandera gharera mata

"**Then this girl made Rasālā (a kind of juice) Mathāni, rock candy, Maāḍa (gruel) and other preparations. Thus, without any endeavour, Nanda's house became like the abode of the goddess of fortune.**"

dadhi dugdha koto,   āra gābī ghṛta
  naola navanī chānā
nārikela jala,   korolo śītala,
  navīna vāsane pānā

"**She made cool drinks like yoghurt, milk, coconut-juice, whey with fresh butter and cow's *ghi* and poured them into new vessels.**"

āmrera ācāra,   kotoko prakāra,
  kalā pāṅiphala ādā
bhājane bhariyā,   rākhilo ḍhākiyā
  rāṅīra manera sādhā

"**Then she filled vessels with so many kinds of mango-pickles, bananas and waterfruits and covered them, in accordance with Queen Yaśodā's wish.**"

sabhe kore kāma,   nā kore viśrāma,
  ānande ākula cita
eka tāna hoiyā,   madhura koriyā,
  gāota maṅgala gīta

"**Everyone worked untiringly with hearts thrilled with joy, and all the girls sang sweet and auspicious songs in one tune.**"

nija kāja sāri,   sakala sundarī,
*   rāṇīre kohite jāy*
rādhikā dulāri,   dekhite colori,
*   kohoye śekhara rāy*

"All the beautiful girls then told Queen Yaśodā what service they had rendered. Rāy śekhara says: "Now go and see Rādhikā Dulāri!" (29)

šrī-rāga — tāla eka tālā

sugandhi odana,   vividha vyañjana,
*   rādhikā randhana kori*
śāka pāyasādi,   piṣṭaka avadhi,
*   vedira upore dhari*

"Rādhikā cooked fragrant rice and different vegetable-preparations, keeping the *śāka, kṣīra,* cakes and so on the table."

sahasra prakāra,   vyañjana ācāra,
*   rāi samāpana kori*
goṭhete hoite,   sakhāra sahite,
*   ghare re āilā hari*

"Rāi prepared thousands of kinds of vegetable- and pickle-preparations. Meanwhile Hari and His friends returned home from the meadows."

nandarāṇī kohe,   jāho bāchā sabe,
*   sināna koriyā āsi*
kānura sahite,   parama pirīte,
*   bhojana koribe bosi*

"Nandarāāī (Yaśodā) said: "Go, boys and take a bath! Then you can all sit and eat with Kṛṣṇa in topmost love!"

> *kamala nayāna,*   *korite sināna,*
> > *bosilā vediropare*
> *sāraṅga āsiyā,*   *caraṇa mājiyā,*
> > *porālo sināna cīre*

"Lotus-eyed Kṛṣṇa then sat down on a bathing platform to take His bath. Sāraṅga then came, washed Kṛṣṇa's feet and dressed Him in a bathing dress."

> *raktaka patraka,*   *joteko sevaka,*
> > *kānura sināna tare*
> *sugandhi śītala,*   *nirmala salila,*
> > *vedīra upore dhare*

"All servants, like Raktaka and Patraka, engaged in bathing Kṛṣṇa, pouring fragrant, cool and spotless water over the platform."

> *āni madhu kaṇṭha,*   *udvartana jhāṭa,*
> > *mardana koroye aṅge*
> *madana mohana,*   *koroye sināna,*
> > *sab sakhāgaṇa saṅge*

"Madhukaāṭha quickly brought *udvartana* and massaged Madana Mohana's body with it. Thus Kṛṣṇa bathed together with all His friends."

> *sināna koriyā,*   *gākhāni muchiyā*
> > *porilā je pīta dhoṛā*
> *kānura bhojana,* *sopāna kāraṇa,*
> > *śekhara poṛilo sāṛā*

"After bathing Kṛṣṇa, the servants dried off His body and dressed Him in His yellow *dhoti*. Rāya śekhara then called Kṛṣṇa for His meal." (30)

❦

rāginī dhānaśī — tāla eka tālā

bhojana mandira,   bhitora bāhira,
            śodhiyā śītala kori
piṇḍā sāri sāri,   suvarṇa jhājhari,
            sugandhi salila bhori

."In the dining room, which was cleansed and cooled inside out, golden goblets filled with fragrant water stood ready on rows of small low tables."

rāi sakhīgaṇa,   joteko miṣṭānna,
            kramaye koriyā rākhi
se sab vināṇī,   nandera gharaṇī
            dekhiyā hoilā sukhī

"Rāi and Her *sakhīs* gradually placed all the sweets in their place, and when Nanda's wife Yaśodā saw this arrangement she became happy."

kānāi bolāi,   mili dona bhāi,
            sakhāgaṇa kori saṅge
bhojane bosiyā,   pakānna dekhiyā,
            baṭur bāṛhilo raṅge

"The two brothers Kānāi (Kṛṣṇa) and Balāi (Balarāma) met, joined together with Their cowherd boyfriends and sat down to eat. When Baṭu (Madhumaṅgala) saw the cooked rice, his joy increased."

rohiṇī-nandana,   koroye bhojana,
kānura ḍāhine bosi,
vāmete subala,   sammukhe maṅgala,
saghane uṭhaye hāsi

"Rohiāī-nandana Balarāma sat on Kṛṣṇa's right, Subala sat on His left and Madhumaṅgala faced Him as He ate. Great laughter then arose."

rāmera jananī,   dichen āpani,
rādhikā rāndhilā yoto,
sugandhi odana,   vividha vyañjana,
tāhā vā kohibo koto

"How can I describe all the dishes, like fragrant rice and different vegetable-preparations mother Rohiāī and Rādhikā had cooked and were serving?"

vidhi agocara,   yoto upahāra,
dichena rohiṅī māy
rādhāra vadana,   dekhi acetana,
hoilā nāgara rāy

"Even the Creator cannot imagine how many dishes Mother Rohiāī was serving! I see that Nāgara Rāya (Kṛṣṇa) has fainted after seeing Rādhā's face!"

aruci dekhiyā,   ākula hoiyā,
kohoye nandera rāṅī,
rādhā rasavatī,   karpūra mālatī,
tomāra lāgiyā āni

"Nandarāāī Yaśodā became very upset when she saw Kṛṣṇa's lack of appetite, so she said: "I have brought

the great cook, the beautiful young girl Rādhā especially to cook for You!"

tumi nā khāile,   rāi nā āsibe,
svarūpa kohilām tore,
viśākhā lalitā,   āra kundalatā,
ṭhāriyā kohiche more

"I tell You truly, if You don't eat Rāi will not come anymore! Viśākhā, Lalitā and Kundalatā have hinted that to me!"

māyera vacane,   pāolo cetana,
nāgara śekhara kān
rāiye sukha diyā,   ākaṇṭha pūriyā,
korolo bhojana pān

"When Nāgara śekhara, Kṛṣṇa, the king of amorous heroes, heard these words of His mother, He filled Himself upto the neck with food and drinks, to Rāi's pleasure."

sab sakhāgaṇe,   koriyā bhojane
uṭhilā āpana sukhe
ācamana kori,   jāy gaṛāgaṛi,
karpura tāmbūla mukhe

"After eating all the cowherd boys blissfully got up, washed their mouths and placed camphor-laced betel leaves in their mouths, prodding each other and jumping over each other."

nandera nandana,   kori ācamana,
pālaṅke ḍhālilo gā

caraṇa sevana,   kore dāsa gaṇa
  śekhara koroye bā

"Nanda's son then washed His mouth and reclined on His bed (to digest His food). Rāya śekhara praises the servants that sit down to massage His feet." (31)

śrī rādhāra bhojana
rāginī dhānaśī — tāla eka tālā

randhana malinī,   hoiyā ramanī,
  bāhire hoiyā bosi
ghāme ṭalamala, se aṅga atula,
  jemona divase śaśi

"Tired of cooking, Rāi came out of the kitchen and sat down. Her matchless body, that resembles a daytime-moon, was shivering and perspiring."

āsi dāsīgaṇa, dhoyāya caraṇa,
  sugandhi śītala nīre
priya sakhīgaṇa, porāya vasana,
  charama korāya dūre

"Then Her maidservants came and washed Her lotus feet with fragrant and cold water. Her dear girlfriends dressed Her in new garments and relieved Her fatigue."

rādhāra dāsīgaṇa, parama nipuṇa,
  mājiyā virala ghare
bosite āsana, jalera bhājana,
  sāri sāri kori dhare

"Rādhā's maidservants, who are most expert, seated Her on an *āsana* in a solitary room, holding rows of waterpots in their hands."

> *jaśodā ākuli,   koriyā bikuli,*
> *raiere korolo kole*
> *o mora bāchani,   yānmu nichani,*
> *bhojana koroho bole*

"Mother Yaśodā then anxiously took Rāi on her lap and said: "O my daughter! I pray to You: eat something!""

> *rānīra vacana   colilā bhojane,*
> *bosilā āsanopari*
> *rohinī āniyā,   dena jogāiyā*
> *thālite thālite bhori*

"On the request of Queen Yaśodā, śrī Rādhikā proceeded by sitting on an *āsana* to eat. Rohiāī then brought in plate after plate of food."

> *rādhāra ye paṅa,   ānilā tokhon,*
> *kundalatā priyatamā*
> *avaśeṣa loiyā,   dilena āniyā,*
> *koriyā cāturī sīmā*

"Dearmost Kundalatā then brought Rādhā's price, showing the limit of dexterity by bringing Her (Kṛṣṇa's) remnants."

> *sakhīgaṇa saṅge,   nānā rasa raṅge,*
> *bhojana koroho sukhe*
> *bhakṣya samāpana,   kori ācamana,*
> *tāmbūla deolo mukhe*

"**Śrī Rādhikā blissfully took Her meal, having different kinds of** *rasika* **fun with Her girlfriends. After completing Her meal She flushed Her mouth and (the** *kiṅkarīs*) **placed a** *pān* **in Her mouth.**"

pālaṅka upari,   bosilā sundarī,
bāliśe helāno diyā
rāiyera iṅgite,   ye chilo thālite,
bhuñjalo śekhara giyā

"**Beautiful Rādhikā sat down on a couch and leaned against a cushion. On Rāi's indication   Rāya śekhara ate all that was left on Her plate.**" (32)

❀

vrajeśvarī kartṛk śrī rādhāra veśa vinyāsa
rāginī tuḍi — tāla eka tālā

ulāli dulāli,   sohāge āguli,
kohiyā sājāya rāṅī
cāṅcara cikura,   mājalo sundara,
bāndhalo vicitra veṅī

"**Blissfully and affectionately Queen Yaśodā called Rādhā to dress and ornament Her. She tied a wonderful braid of Her beautiful curly locks.**"

ki nā se rāṅīra sādhā
navīna vasane,   bhūṣaṇe maṇḍita,
koyoli sundarī rādhā

"**What did Queen Yaśodā not endeavour, decorating Sundarī Rādhā with fresh clothes and new ornaments?**"

udaya aruṅa, garava garāsi,
sithāra sindūra khāni
tilaka alaka, lalake jhalaka,
palake mohoye muni

"She put *sindūra* (a vermilion stripe) in Rādhā's part that destroys the pride of the (red) rising sun. Then she put shimmering *tilaka* on Her forehead that enchants even the Munis (sages) in a twinkle."

kājale sājalo, nayana yugala,
mājilo sundara mukh
bhurura bhaṅgimā, baṅkimā dekhite,
kāmera kāṁpaye buk

"Yaśodā decorated Rādhā's eyes with collyrium that inundated Her beautiful face (with the aura of its luster). Even Cupid gets heart-throbs when he sees the crooked movements of Her eyebrows."

nāsāra upora, vicitra veśara,
niśvāse saghane dole
parama jatane, puruṣa ratane
parāṅa sahita khele

"She hung a wonderful nose-ring in Her nose, that dangled along with Her breath. The jewel of men (Kṛṣṇa) will most attentively play with that."

kāne kāna phula, atula amūla,
chaṭāya ghaṭāya ravi
heriyā vikala, anaṅga ākula,
roholo tāhāte sevi

"She placed incomparible, priceless flowers in Rādhikā's ears, that shine like the sun. When Cupid sees this he becomes agitated and remains engaged in their service."

cibuka cikaṅa,   kāmera bhājana,
tāhāte kasturi bindu
daśana vasana,   bhuvana mohana,
vacana amiyā sindhu

"Then she placed a drop of musk on Rādhikā's shining chin, which is the abode of Cupid. Her lips captivate the world and Her words are an ocean of nectar."

candane carcita,   parama pavitra,
pīna payodhara joṛa
kaṣita kañculi,   tāhāte jhāṁpali,
bāndhali atula ḍora

"She rubbed Her big breasts with the purest sandalwood pulp and then covered them with a pure blouse, binding it with matchless straps!"

prabāle prabala,   korolo māla,
bhālo kālo puṅti jyoti
hema hīrā maṅi,   vicitra vināni
tāhāte deolo moti

"She made a garland of powerful coral and nicely effulgent black beads for Her forehead and made a wonderful braid of Her hair, placing gold, diamonds, jewels and pearls in it."

se je jaśomati,   pirīti mūrati,
rāire koriyā kole

se sab bhūṣaṅa,   koriyā jatana
deyolo tāhāra gole

"This Yaśomati, who is the embodiment of love, then took Rāi on her lap and carefully placed all these ornaments around Her neck."

hiye hīra hāra,   ati manohara,
tāhāte padaka sāje
dekhi dinamaṅi,   catura āpani,
kiraṅa lukāya lāje

"She hung a string of highly enchanting diamonds around Her neck, with a locket in the middle. When the sun (who is the gem of the day) beheld such expertise, he shyly concealed his rays."

rāmā kāma-śālā,   śaṅkha śaśikalā,
śobhaye se bhuja āge
ratana kaṅkaṅa,   kiṅkiṅī jhaṅkaṅa,
anaṅge camaka lāge

"She beautified śrī Rādhikā's wrists with moonbeam-ivory bangles that are the abodes of erotic incitement, and gave Her jewelled armlets and jingling waistbells that astonished Cupid."

tāṛa gāṛa sāja,   gati kāma rāja,
deolo rāiko bhuje
vipakṣa mardani,   mudrikā khecani,
anguli upori sāje

"She placed *tāḍa* and *gāḍa* armlets on Rāi's arms, that arouse king Cupid. Then she placed the jewel-studded

**(*khecani*) ring called Vipakṣa Mada Mardani (the destroy-
er of Cupid's pride) on Rāi's finger."**

> *jalada paṭala,　　　　garava garāsi,*
> *　　pohirī nīlima vāsa*
> *kiṅkiṅī śabade,　　　　javada korolo,*
> *　　kaṭake caṭaka bhāṣa*

**"She dressed Rāi in a blue *sārī* that defeats the
pride of a host of rain clouds, and with waist-bells and
bangles that defeat the sounds of Cataka birds."**

> *mañjīra puñjali,　　koriyā jatana,*
> *　　śekhara porāya pāy*
> *jaśodā rohiṅī,　　samukhe āpani,*
> *　　sājaolo saba gāy*

**"Rāya śekhara assists by carefully hanging ankle-
bells on Rāi's feet. Yaśodā and Rohiāī thus decorated Rāi's
whole body right in front of me!" (33)**

⁂

> *jaśodā rohiṅī,　　parama jatane*
> *　　sājāolo sab sakhī*
> *sundara sindūra,　　kaṭaka ṭhāṭaka*
> *　　lāgalo kāmera āṅkhi*

**"With topmost care Yaśodā and Rohiāī thus deco-
rated all the *sakhīs* with beautiful vermilion and a host of
armlets that caught the eye of Cupid."**

> *jaśodā antara,　　amiyā sāgara,*
> *　　rādhikā makara tāy*

agama athala   madhura śītala,
    ḍubalo sakala gāy

"Yaśodā's heart is like an ocean of nectar and Rādhikā is a Makara-fish that swims in it. Her whole body is immersed in this boundless, deep, sweet and cool ocean."

āmāra jīvana,   toṁarā du jana,
    dukhāni āṅkhira tārā
vraja rāja mana,   jānibā emon
    se jana āmāri pārā

"You Two (Kṛṣṇa and Rādhikā) are my very life and the two pupils in my two eyes, and You should know that the mind of Vraja Rāja Nanda is similar to mine."

e ghara karaṅa,   todera kāraṅa,
    śunaho rājāra jhī
dhātāra māthāya,   poṛuka bajara,
    āra vā bolibo kī

"Listen, O princess of mine! You are the cause of this whole household being run! Let a thunderbolt fall on the Creator's head (for You not being my daughter-in-law)— what more can I say?"

āra kibā kohu,   tomā heno bahu
    nāhiko āmāra ghare
hiyāy āguni,   uṭhiche dvi guṅi
    ki āra kohibo tore

"What more can I say (about My agony)? I don't have a daughter-in-law like You in my house. The fire in my heart doubles in intensity — what more can I tell You?"

jaṭilā kupile,　　āsite nā dibe,
*　　se āra āpada doṛo*
kuṭilā kumati,　　viṣera mūrati,
*　　seho se dhāuṛa boṛo*

"There is one more thing I fear— When Jaṭilā becomes angry she will not allow You to come anymore. The foolish Kuṭilā is the embodiment of poison — she is also a big upstart."

dineka soyāthe,　　nāriye rākhite,
*　　tāhāre hoilo ḍoṛo*
niśvāse chutuṇā,　　koroye ghaṭanā,
*　　se boṛo viṣama ghara*

"I can not remain calm for even a day out of fear of them. In that greatly unbearable house one fears even breathing out by chance."

durmedha āyāna,　　se ati durjana,
*　　nā jāni kemona cīta*
śekhara minati,　　śuno yaśomati,
*　　sabhāra ekoi rīta*

"Who knows what is on the mind of this greatly wicked and foolish āyāna (Rādhā's husband)?" Rāya Śekhara humbly submits to mother Yaśodā: "Listen— they are all of the same nature!" (34)

❀

rāgiāī sindhuḍā — tāla daśa kusi

o mora bāchani dhani,　　satīkula śiromaṇi,
*　　kṣaṇeka viśrāma koro sukhe*

nā hoye uchara belā,   sakhīgaṇa koro khelā,
    karpūra tāmbūla dāo mukhe

"O my precious little girl, O crestjewel of chaste girls, happily take rest for a while. It is not so late, so play a little with Your friends and enjoy some betelleaves with camphor!"

rūpa guṇa kāja tora,   parāṇa nichani mora,
    śutiyā svapane dekhi sadā
tomā heno guṇa nidhi,   āmāre nā dilā vidhi,
    hṛdaye rahiyā gelā sādhā

"Your form, qualities and activities soothe my heart and I always dream of them when I sleep. My heart feels pain when I wonder why Fate did not bestow an ocean of virtues like You upon me."

dhātāra māthāye bāj,   ye heno koriyā kāj,
    āmāre bhaṅgilā kibā doṣe
bāchāra vivāha tāre,   heno nāri nāhi pure,
    cāhiyā nā pāi kon deśe

"Let a thunderbolt fall on the head of the Creator (Fate) for doing this! What wrong have I done to be devoid of a daughter like You? I cannot find any girl in the whole area as suitable to marry to my boy as You!"

yaśodāra viṣāda kothā,   śuni vṛṣabhānu sutā,
    vadane vasana diyā hāse
pulake pūralo gā,   mukhe nā niḥsare rā,
    bhāsilo nārīra sneha rase

"Hearing Yaśodā's sad words, Vṛṣabhānu's daughter laughed naughtily, covering Her smile with Her veil.

Both were floating in the nectar stream of female affection, their bodies studded with goose bumps and their mouths unable to make any sound."

śekhara sarasa kori,   kohe śuno vrajeśvarī,
rādhikā tomāra heno jāni
sakhā sab pūre veṅu,   kharike ḍākiche dhenu,
sājāo gā rākhāl śiromaṇi

"Rāy Śekhara says in a *rasika* way: "Hear me, O Queen of Vraja! You should know that Rādhikā is yours! The cowherd friends are all filling the holes of their flutes and the cows are bellowing in the meadows! Decorate Your body now, O crownjewel of cowherds! (35)

purvāhna kāla- atha goṣṭha gamanaṁ
śrī kṛṣṇer veśa vinyāsa
rāginī bhāṭiyāri — tāla daśa kusi

sumukhi saṇketa jāni,   turite colilā rāṇī,
āsiyā pośilā veśa ghare
kānure āniyā tathi,   veśa kore jaśomati,
dukhe hiyā dara dara kore

"While Sumukhi (beautiful faced Rāi) interpreted Yaśodā's words, Queen Yaśodā quickly went to Kṛṣṇa's dressing room. Bringing Kṛṣṇa in she dressed Him, her heart throbbing of anguish."

nanda-rāṇī kāch kāce nāṭuyāra chānde
ṭāniyā bāndhalo cūḍā,   nava guñjā diyā beṛā
tāhe dilo śikhi puccha cāṇde (dhru.)

"When this king of dancers came to Nandarāāī, she bound a crown on His head (or: she bound a top knot of hair on His head), surrounded it with a string of fresh *guñjā* berries and stuck a peacock feather in it."

*kibā se grīvāra śobhā,   madanera manolobhā
gorocanā tilaka subhāle
hiye hāra maṇi jvale,   vanamālā dole gole,
amūlya mukutā nāsātale*

"Behold the beauty of Kṛṣṇa's neck — it is tempting even Cupid's mind! He got a *tilaka* of *gorocana* on His beautiful forehead, a shimmering jewel necklace on His chest, and a garland of forest flowers around His neck, and a precious pearl was made to dangle from His nose."

*aṅgada balayā kore,   śobhiyāche thare thare,
candane cikana kālā tanu
porāilo pīta dhoṛā,   tāhāte ghāgar beṛā
coloite kore runu jhunu*

"He got beautiful bangles on His wrists, sandalwood paste anointed on His glossy black body, a yellow *dhoti* on His hips, with a belt of bells hanging over it, that jingle as He walks."

*rātula dhoṛāra thope,   du dige nāmiyā śobhe,
baṅkarāj sane kore melā
khone khone uṛe bāy,   āsiyā lāgaye pāy,
nūpura sahite kore khelā*

"Two red tassles were beautifully suspended from this in two directions, meeting with His Baṅkarāja foot-ornaments. At some moments the breeze blew and caused them to reach down to His feet and play with His ankle-bells."

> *ḍākinī sākinī bhoye,   dhore prāṇ nāhi roye,*
> *bādiyā sādhiyā āni māy*
> *ajara amara tanu,   hoye jeno rāma kānu*
> *emoti bāndhiyā dibe gāy*

"Life did not remain in Mother Yaśodā's body out of fear of witches and ghosts, so she brought amulets which she bound so firmly to Balarāma and Kṛṣṇa's bodies that They became as if free from death and disease."

> *bādiyā sādhana pori,   bāndhe rakṣā maṇi poṛhi,*
> *rāma dāmodara ḍekhi hāse*
> *daṇḍavat kori māy,   rāma dāmodara jāy,*
> *yaśodā rohiṇī tāra pāśe*

"After placing the amulets she also tied protective stones on Them. When Rāma and Dāmodara saw this, They laughed and offered prostrated obeisances at her feet. Then They went out, flanked by Yaśodā and Rohiāī."

> *rohiyā rohiyā jāy,   phiriyā phiriyā cāy*
> *jananī prabodhe bāre bāre*
> *śekhara śunoho bol,   ki lāgiyā koro rol,*
> *māyere loiyā jāo ghore*

"As Kṛṣṇa walked along He kept on looking back, repeatedly consoling His mother. Hear the words of Rāy śekhara— "Why do You speak so much? Just take Your mother into the house!" (36)

gostha yātrā

hiyāya āguni bharā,   āṅkhi bohe bahu dhārā,
dukhe buka vidariyā yāy
ghara para je nā jāne,   se janā colilā vane,
e tāpa kemone sahe jāy

"My heart is filled with fire and many streams (of tears) flow from my eyes. My heart is breaking of misery! He who does not know the difference between His home and the outside is going to the forest. How can this scorching be tolerated?"

ore mora jīvana dulāliyā!
kibā ghare nāhi dhana,   keno vā jāibe vana,
rākhāla rākhibe dhenu loiyā (dhru)

"O Child of My heart! Don't we have enough wealth in the house already? Why do You have to go to the forest then? Let the cowherdboys go out with the cows into the forest!"

āge pāche nāhi morā,   hāputira put torā,
āndhala koriyā jābi more
dudhera chāoyāla hoiyā,   vane jābe dhenu loiyā,
ki dekhi rahibo āmi ghare?

"I don't know anyone else but You—You are My only son, so if You accidentally become hurt I'll be driven blind! Being my suckling boy, why are You taking Your cows into the forest? Can I just remain at home, peacefully watching it?"

nanī jini tanukhāni,   ātape milāya jāni
se bhaye saghane prāṇa kāṁpe
bāṛava anala pārā,   viṣama ravira kharā,
kemone sahibe heno tāpe?

"Your body is even softer than butter! My heart shivers of deep fear when I think what will happen when the harsh sunrays will touch You. How will You tolerate such heat?"

kuśera aṅkura boṛo,   śelera samāna doṛo,
śunite siñciṛā poṛe gāy
śirīṣa kusuma dala,   jiniyā caraṇatala,
kemone dhāibe heno pāy

"I'm afraid the big Kuśa-grassroots will hurt You like javelins. Hearing it I sprinkle my body (with tears). How will Your footsoles, that are more tender than śirīṣa-flowerpetals, run over this ground?"

māyera karuṇā vāṇī,   śuniyā gokula maṇi,
koto mate māyere bujhāya.
viṣāda nā koro mone,   kichu bhay nāhi vane,
ithe sāthi e śekhara rāya

"Hearing His mother's pitiful words, Gokula-maāi Kṛṣṇa explained His mother in so many ways: "Don't be sad at heart! There's nothing to fear in the forest!", and Rāya śekhara is the witness! (37)

mātṛ sambodhana

dhariyā māyera kara,   kohe rāma dāmodara,
śubha kāje nā koriho dukha

āmāra kulera dharma,   gocāraṇa nija karma,
*   korite pāi je boṛo sukha*

"Holding mother Yaśodā's hands, Balarāma and Dāmodara told her: "Don't be unhappy at the good work We are performing. It is our dynastic duty to herd cows and Our job makes Us very happy."

hā bolā goyāla jāti,   śṛgāla dekhilo kati,
*   se bhoy āsiyā koilo tore*
gharera samāna bona,   corāibo dhenugaṇa
*   dādāra sahite nāhi ḍore*

"You are afraid that We will go out like foolish cowherd boys that ignore the presence of so many jackals. The forest where We tend Our cows is like home to Us— in big brother Balarāma's presence there is no fear."

keho kon kothā kohe,   se sakala sācā nohe
*   svapaneho nā śuno śravaṇe*
svarūpe kohiluṅ kothā,   niścoy jāniho mātā
*   asura nāhiko ār bone*

"Whatever people say is untrue— don't listen to them even in your dreams! I tell you in truth, O mother, and rest assured— there are no more demons left in the forest!"

govardhane dhenu melā,   sabhāi korigo khelā,
*   dhaniṣṭhā jāibe sei khāne*
tomāra bhojana kothā,   āmāre kohibe tathā
*   tabe se koribo jala pāne*

"We play with Our cows near Mount Govardhana. Let Dhaniṣṭhā go there to tell Us that you have taken your

meal. Only when I have heard that I shall (eat and) drink water."

śekharera śuno bol,   keho nā koriho gol
māyere loiyā jāo ghare
ye jan catura hoy,   tāhāre bujhāyā loy
bujhiyā āpana kāja kore

"Hear Rāya Śekhara's words — let no one cause confusion. Take mother home. Anyone who is intelligent should understand that everyone must perform his own duty." (38)

꧁

dūtīr cāturī
rāga— sāraṇga

nandera gharaṇī,   śunoho kāhinī,
turite coloho ghore
rāiyera vilamba,   hoile jaṭilā,
viṣama jāni se kore

(A *dūtī* said:) "O wife of Nanda! Hear me! Quickly return home! I know that Jaṭilā becomes terrifying if Rāi returns home late."

sājāyā kāchāyā,   rādhāre loiyā,
jāuk tomāra loke
jaṭilā tomāra,   dekhiyā vebhāra,
bharasā bāndhuka buke

"Let Rādhā go home after dressing and ornament-ing. May Jaṭilā get faith in you when she sees your behav-iour."

> *kuṭilā kumati,   sadāi kurīti,*
> *chidra cāhiyā bule*
> *boṛo se dhāuṛi,   kothāra bāguṛi*
> *koṇete bosiyā tole*

"The foolish and wicked Kuṭilā constantly wanders around looking for faults. She is very shameless and talkative and sits in a corner, spreading a network of gossip."

> *śuniyā vacana,   colilā bhavana,*
> *kānure vidāya diyā*
> *śekhara hāsiyā,   nāgare ṭhāriyā,*
> *rāṇīre colilo loiyā*

"Hearing these words, mother Yaśodā granted leave to Kṛṣṇa and returned home. Laughing, Rāy śekhara gave a hint to Nāgara Kṛṣṇa and took Queen Yaśodā home." (39)

❀

sāraṅga rāga / boḍāri — tāla daśa kusi

> *jananī vidāy kori,   goṭhete colilā hari;*
> *kohoye śuno re ore bhāi*
> *nā jāibo kon māṭhe,   colu sabe giritaṭe*
> *hāṅkāiyā deho sab gāi*

"Taking leave from His mother, Hari went into the meadows, saying: "O brother! We won't go to any meadow, let's go to the base of Govardhana Hill! Call all the cows!"

> *govinda kuṇḍera jal,   manohara suśītal,*
> *tṛṇa saba āche sukomala*

tāhe dhenu niyojiyā,   khelibo bulibo jāiyā
dekhibo kemon giritala

"The water of Govinda Kuāḍa is enchanting and cool and all the grass there is very soft. There we will graze our cows and wander around playing, admiring the beauty of the base of Govardhana Hill."

śuniyā bolāi sukhe,   śingā diyā cāṇda mukhe
dhavalī sāolī boli ḍāke
pisaṇgi maṇika stani,   boli ḍāke guṇamaṇi,
dhenu sab cālāilo hāke

"Hearing this, Balāi (Balarāma) blissfully placed His horn at His moon-like mouth and called the cows Dhavali and śābali with it. Guāamaāi Kṛṣṇa then called the cows Piśaṇgi and Maāikastani and then drove them along with all the others."

keho nāce keho gāya, keho batsa pāche dhāya
ghāṇgara nūpura kore dhvani
taruṇa tarṇaka yoto,   tārā bhelo unamata
dhāya saba śuniyā se dhvani

"Some cowherdboys were dancing, some were singing and some were running behind the calves, making their waistbells and anklebells jingling. Hearing this sound, all the young calves became mad with joy and came running."

ūrdvha karṇa ūrdhva puccha,   ghūrṇita nayāne batsa
dhāiyā pośilā govardhane
rām dāmodara saṇge,   jāy śiśu mahāraṇge
dhenu phirāilo jane jane

"With raised ears, raised tails and rolling eyes the calves ran to Mount Govardhana. The cowherd boys then blissfully returned the cows in the company of Balarāma and Dāmodara (Kṛṣṇa)."

rām kohe ore bhāi,   eikhāne coruk gāi
āiso sobāi kori khelā
tṛṇe niyojiyā dhenu,   khelā khele rām kānu,
heriyā śekhara mana bholā

"Balarāma said: O brother, let the cows graze here. Come now all of you and let's play." When Rāy śekhara thus sees the cows grazing and Balarāma and Kṛṣṇa playing, he becomes overwhelmed by transcendental bliss." (40)

rāgiāī dhānaśī — tāla eka tālā

sab dhenugaṇa loiyā,   gopane niyojiyā
sabāre korilo sābadhān
dādār nikaṭe jāiyā,   binoye vidāy hoiyā,
vana-śobhā dekhibāre kān

"Kṛṣṇa took all the cows along and engaged all the cowherd boys, warning them to take good care of them. Then He went to His elder brother (Balarāma) and humbly took leave of Him on the pretext of admiring the beauty of the forest."

kānu kohe ore bhāi,   khelo sabe ei ṭhāi
āmi āsi kānana dekhiyā
thākibe dādār kāche,   keho kothā jāo pāche
gilibe asure sobe loiye

"Kṛṣṇa said: O brother, why don't you all keep playing here? I'm going to see the beauty of the forest. All you boys stay close to Dādā (My elder brother Balarāma)! If someone stays behind a demon may come and swallow you all!"

śiśu paśu niyojiyā,   śubala baṭure loiyā
bāhira hoilā naṭa-rāy
rāiyer sarasī kule,   āilā kadamba tale,
somoye śekhara rasa gāy

"After thus engaging the boys and the cattle, Naṭa Rāy (Kṛṣṇa, the monarch of actors) went out with Subala and Madhumaṅgala, thus reaching the base of a Kadamba-tree on the bank of Rādhākuāḍa. Knowing the time, Rāy śekhara sings this *rasika* (succulent) song." (41)

❁

yaśodā vilāpa
rāginī suhai — tāla teoṭa

kānure pāṭhāiyā bone,   jaśodā biṣāda mone,
āsiyā rādhikā kori kore
dukhe āulāiche gā,   mukhe na niḥsore rā
vasana bhijiyā gelo lore

"Mother Yaśoda was full of sorrow after sending Kṛṣṇa into the forest, so she came and took Rādhikā on her lap. Her body was tormented by misery, her mouth could not utter one word and her dress was soaked with tears."

gada gada svare rāṇī,   kohoye viṣāda vāṇī,
dhariyā rādhār duṭi kore

kīrtidā samāna heno,   āmāre jānibā teno,
se ghor e ghor sab tore

"With faltering voice Queen Yaśodā held Rādhā's hands and spoke the following sad words— "See me as non-different from Your mother Kīrtidā — this house is Yours, just as Your own home!"

ki ār koribo sādh,   sakale poṛilo bād,
dinek rākhite nāri tomā
emani biṣam lok,   jīyante pāṛaye pok,
tileka nāhiko kāru khamā

"What more can I do? Everyone speaks (slander). I cannot even keep You for one day! Such harsh people are living around here. Nobody has even the slightest compassion!"

vividha modaka rāṇ   rāiyera āñcale āni,
dilā koto jatana koriyā
phukāra koriyā kāṇde,   hiyā thira nāhi bāndhe,
dhārā bohe mukha buka bāhiyā

"Very carefully Queen Yaśodā bound different sweets in the border of Rāi's garment. She wept loudly and could not remain calm— tears streamed over her face and her breasts."

rāṇīra karuṇā śuni,   pāṣāṇa goloye jāni,
sakhīgaṇa kāndiyā bethita
śekhara somoy jāni,   thira koilo nanda-rāṇī,
kohe rāi coloho turite

"Hearing Queen Yaśodā's pitiful cries the stones melted and the *sakhīs* wept with great pain. Knowing the

**time proper, Rāy śekhara consoled Nanda-rāāī and told
Rāi: "Come on, let's go quickly!" (42)**

rāginī ṭori — tāla gaḍakhemaṭā

kundalatā sane kothā kohe nandarāṇī;
rāire loiyā bāchā coloho āpani
jatana koriyā badhū sompibe tāhāre;
kohibe sakal kothā binoy vebhāre
jaṭilā tomāre boṛo kore paratīt;
bujhiyā kohibe tāre je hoy ucit
rādhikā āmār jeno niti āise jāy;
lalitā viśākhā loiyā koribe upāy

**"Nandarāṇi Yaśodā told Kundalatā: "O daughter
of mine! Go and take Rāi with you. Carefully place her
daughter-in-law in Jaṭilā's hand. Always speak and behave
with her in a humble way; Jaṭilā has a lot of faith in you—
properly explain her all that happened. May my Rādhikā
always nicely come to my house and may She always take
Her assistants Lalitā and Viśākhā along."**

bidāy korite nāre kāndaye karuṇe;
mukhāni dhariyā cumba dey ghane ghane
stana-khīr dhāre aṅga koroye siñcan;
krome krome lālana korilā sakhīgaṅ
rāṇīra caraṇa-dhūli sabe loilo śire;
nandera mahal hoite hoilo bāhire
śekhar kohoye hiyā samvarite nāre;
pāchu pāchu gamana korilo koto dūre

**Mother Yaśodā could not properly grant leave to
śrī Rādhikā — she simply stood there, weeping pitifully.**

Holding Rādhikā's face she kissed Her again and again, all the while showering Her with her breast milk (that squirted out of her breasts out of motherly love). Then she also gradually fondled all of śrī Rādhikā's *sakhīs*. All the girls then took Queen Yaśodā's foot-dust on their heads and left Nanda's palace. Rāy śekhara says: "Mother Yaśodā could not control her feelings — she followed them for a long way." (43)

dhānaśī — tāla eka tālā lophā

> *kānane gamana korolo jaba kān;*
> *dhani soye sanket muralī niśāna*
> *kalāvatī kauśala kohone nā jāy;*
> *praṇati korolo puna jaśomati pāya*
> *anumati māgai anunoy koroi;*
> *vrajapati dampati animikhe rohoi*
> *gadgada śabade nā phuraye vāṇī;*
> *gara gara antara puna dhoru pāṇi*
> *tuhuṅ ati guṇamaṇī koroho payān;*
> *āndhalo bhoi gelo hāmāri nayān*
> *ākule anusari āoli dūr;*
> *kātare kamalinī kohoi madhura*
> *minati koriyā dhani rāṇī bāhuṛai;*
> *koho kavi śekhara bahu caturāi*

"When Kṛṣṇa went to the forest He played His flute to give a sign to fortunate Rāi. Kalāvatī's expertise is indescribable; again She offered Her obeisances unto mother Yaśodā's lotusfeet and humbly begged her for permission. The wife of the king of Vraja stared at Her without blinking and could not find proper words to say. Her words faltered and with a palpitating heart she held Rāi's hand again, anxiously speaking the following sweet words to Kamalinī (lotus-like) Rāi: "O most qualified jewel of girls! You may leave now— my eyes now see nothing but darkness! You have come from so far with so much eagerness!" Then the Queen humbly asked fortunate Rāi to come back again (the next day). Kavi śekhara says: "There is a lot of cleverness going on here." (44)

❁

śrī rādhār gṛhe gamana
śrī rāga — tāla lophā

sakhī sāthe cole pathe rāi vinodinī;
viṣāde vyākula hoiyā kohoye kāhinī
e nārī janame hām koilo koto pāpa;
sei phale sadāi pāiye manastāpa
nanadinī kuvādinī prati bole bhāje;
śāśuṛī saghana more āṅkhi ṭhāre tāje
svāmī sohāge kabhu nā ḍākilo more;
niśvāsa chāṛite nāri devarera ḍore
poṛā se pāṛār loka dekhiyā ḍorāi;
āpanā boliyā bole heno keho nāi
parādhīnī hoiyā prema koinu pora sone;
jāniyā śuniyā jhāṁp diyāchi āguṇe
e kavi śekhara kohe nā koriho ḍor;
gopate bhuñjibe sukha nā bhāviho por

"As Rāi Vinodinī was on Her way with Her *sakhīs* She was agitated by sorrow and said: "How many sins have I committed in this female birth, so that I have to go through all this mental anguish? My sister-in-law is always slandering Me, and My mother-in-law is always keeping a watchful eye on Me. My husband never calls Me with affection, and I am so scared of My brother-in-law that I

74

dare not even breathe. I am afraid even to look at the local villagers! In short, I have no one to call My own. Being thus subdued by My relatives I have fallen in love with another man. Thus I have knowingly and willingly jumped into the fire." Kavi śekhara says: "Do not fear— You will enjoy in secret— do not fear others." (45)

rāga - dhānaśī

> *grāma hi jāvaṭa,   joichana pābaka,*
> *toichano saba jana rīta*
> *para caracā vine,   ānahi nāhi jāne,*
> *nā bujhiye koiche carita*

"Just as the village of Yāvaṭa is like fire, so is the behaviour of all its inhabitants. People don't know anything but slander— their activities are incomprehensible."

> *sakhi re iha kule iha bevahāra*
> *kuṭila kumati jana,   poiśuna parāyaṇa*
> *ninduka gole dhoru hāra*

"O *sakhi*! How this family is behaving! Crooked miscreants are dedicated to hostility and fault-finders carry such.enmity as garlands around their necks."

> *nija nija jaśa guṇa,   ghoṣaye puna puna*
> *keho kāhu hita nāhi māne*
> *hāmāri karama phale,   bihi bāndhi hāte gole*
> *sompalo tākara thāne*

"They glorify their own virtues time and again, without thinking of anyone else's benefit. The Creator has bound the results of My previous activities around My necks and placed Me in the hands of such people."

janame janame koto,   pāpa koiluṇ śata śata
se sab bhelo āgusār
janamiyā iha puri,   mānuṣa ākāra dhari,
jīvana vadhai hāmār

"How many hundreds of sins haven't I committed, birth after birth? Although I have taken human birth in this abode My life is being killed (destroyed)."

nāri janama kori,   kiye bihi sirajilo
tāhe puna kulavati vāda
tāhe rūpa yauvana,   eka nā hoye ūn
āra tāhe prema sādha

"Why has the Creator created the female species, and on top of that the duties of housewives? On top of that there is youthful beauty and all kinds of aspirations in love..."

pāye pāye saṇkaṭa,   joichana kaṇṭaka,
koiche nibāre nāhi jān
aichana ko hoye,   āpana jāniyā mohe
dui dige rākhaye samān

"At every step there are thorn-like dilemmas, and I don't know how to pull them out (solve them). Whom can I thus consider My own people? I must be equally disposed to both sides."

pohile jānitu jab,   iha dukha pāobo
tab kāhe korobo suleho

rāya śekhara vāṇī,   bhavane coloho dhani,
*   kāhe eto koroho sandeha*

"If I knew in advance that I would suffer so much, then would I ever have started this love affair?" Rāya Śekhara says: "O fortunate girl! Go home! Why should You doubt so much?" (46)

❀

śrī rādhār gṛhāgamana
rāga kadamba/ rāgiāī suhai — tāla eka tālā

dhani kundalatā,   viśākhā lalitā,
*   rāire ānilo ghare*
rādhikā ratana,   koriyā jatana,
*   sompoli jaṭilā kore*

"Dhani (fortunate) Kundalatā, Viśākhā and Lalitā brought Rāi home. Thus they carefully hid the Rādhikā-jewel in Jaṭilā's hands."

vividha bhūṣaṇa,   vicitra vasana,
*   dekhiyā vadhūra aṇge*
sādare ādara,   koriyā sabār,
*   bosālo āpana saṇge*

"Seeing different wonderful garments and orna-ments on the body of Her daughter-in-law, Jaṭilā eagerly and attentively seated all the *sakhīs* close to her."

śuno kundalatā,   kohi sab kothā,
*   jaśodā āmāra jhi*
e ghara se ghara,   sakali tāhāra,
*   niścoy koriyāchi*

"Listen Kundalatā, I will tell you everything—Yaśodā is as dear to me as a daughter. This house and her house -—it is all hers. That I know for sure."

nā dekhi nayane,   nā śuni śravaṇe,
*   bosile uṭhite nāri*
śarīra acala,   sadāi vikala,
*   nā jāni kokhono mori*

"My eyes don't see, my ears don't hear and when I sit down I can't get up anymore. My body is motionless and always agitated. I don't know when I will die."

devatā āśīṣe,   thākuk hariṣe,
*   kolera kowara loiyā*
godhana pālana,   koruka saghana,
*   janama āiyati hoiyā*

"May my dear son remain happy, by the Lord's grace. Let him always remain absorbed in tending his cows, and may Rādhā be a life-long *āiyati* (woman whose husband is still alive)."

śuniyā uttara,   śekhara catura,
*   binoye kohoye vāṇī*
tomāra vacana,   carita calana,
*   sadāi japaye rāṇī*

"Hearing this reply, clever Rāya śekhara humbly said: "Rāāī (Queen Yaśodā) does *japa* of Your words, activities and pastimes." (47)

rāgiāī bhūpāli — tāla eka tālā

catura raṇgiṇī rāi sakhīgaṇa saṇga;
yukati koriyā kore buṛīra sane raṇga
avanata boyāne bosilā tāra kāche;
vadhūre virasa dekhi buṛī ghana puche
āji kene tomāre emon pārā dekhi;
vadana aruṇa āra chala chala āṇkhi

"Thus clever and playfal Rāi and Her *sakhīs* **bliss-fully spoke with Jaṭilā, sitting next to her with lowered heads. Seeing her daughter-in-law in a dejected mood, Jaṭilā asked Her: "Why do I see You so sad today? Your face is red and Your eyes are full of tears."**

kebā ki bolilo tore kene vā emon;
āmāra śapathi lāge kohibe ekhon
śāśuṛī vacana śuni kohe vinodinī;
āpana karama bhoga bhuñjiye āpani

"Has anybody said something to make You feel like this? I swear You, tell me now!" Hearing the words of Her mother-in-law, Vinodinī Rāi said: "Everyone must suffer the results of his own *karma*!**"**

ke mora āpana baṭe kāhāre kohibo;
je jan kohoye tāhā sakali sahibo
sahaje cakṣera bāli hoiyāchi sabhār;
emon pāṛār loka koroye khāṇkāra

"What can I say to anyone about My fate? I will tolerate whatever anyone says. I've naturally become sand in everyone's eyes. This is how village people slander."

āpana māthāra keśa nā pāri bāndhite;
tāhe para ghara jāi randhana korite
boṛār bahurī āmi boṛār jhiyārī;
kula-vadhū tāhe kothā sohite nā pāri
śekhara sarasa kori rāi ere bujhāy;
e bol bolite dhani tore nā juwāy

"I cannot bind the hair on My own head, and on top of that I go to others' homes to cook. I am the daughter-in-law of a noble lady and the daughter of a noble lady. How can a chaste wife tolerate such gossip?" In a *rasika* manner Rāya śekhara explains to Rāi: "O Dhani, You should not speak like that!" (48)

❀

rāgiṇī suhai — tāla gaḍakhemaṭā

jaṭilā bhulilā rāiyera bole;
prabodhe vadhūre loiyā kole
ki bol bolilā rājhāra jhi;
jaśodā śunile bolibe ki?

"Jaṭilā forgot what Rāi said and addressed her daughter-in-law, taking Her on her lap: "Oh my princess, what did You say? What will Yaśodā say if she hears this?"

koto nā ādara koroye more; vividha bhūṣaṇe bhūṣilo tore
tomāre vāchani bolibo ki; jānibā jaśodā āmāra jhi

"See how much affection she gives to me by adorning You with so many different ornaments? O daughter, what can I say to You? Yaśodā does this because You are my daughter(-in-law)."

ki dhana nāhiko tāhāra ghare; koteko rāndhanī rākhite pāre
tāhāra āmāra ekoi ghara; tāre ki jānaye āpana para

"How much wealth doesn't she have at home, and how many cooks can she not employ? Her house and my house are one and the same. What do we know of 'mine' and 'theirs' in connection with them?"

gaṇake gaṇiyā kohilo tāre; tora hāte khāile pramāyu bāḍe
vara dilo tāhe durvāsā muni; tomāra randhana amṛta jini

"After calculating, a soothsayer told Her: 'The lifespan of anyone who eats from Your hand is increased. Durvāsā Muni offered Her this boon—"May Your cooking defeat (the taste of) nectar!"

je khāi se hoy ajarāmare; ei lāgi tore jatana kore
jadi vidhi tore emati koile; e sab āmār bhāgyera phale

"Anyone who eats this will be free from death and disease. This I tell you intently. If the Creator made You like this, then this is all the result of my good fortune."

āpanāra ghare koribe kāj; tāhāte tomāra kisera lāj?
je jana ihāte kohibe kothā; māthāra upore hoibe māthā

"Why should You be shy to work in her abode? Anyone who gossips about this will perish."

o mora jananī tolaho mukha; āyāna śunile pāibe dukha
āsibe jāibe jaśodā kāche; śekhara saṁhati ki bhoy āche

"O my mother, lift Your head! When Abhimanyu, Your husband, hears You he will become unhappy.

Continue going to Yaśodā." Rāy śekhara says: What fear is there?" (49)

❀

rāgiāī suhanī — tāla rūpaka

bujhāiyā vadhūre,   kohoye satvare
deva pūjibāra tare
kṣaṇeko śayana,   koro saba jana,
alasa koroho dūre

"After instructing her daughter-in-law like this, Jaṭilā urged Her to hurry to prepare for Her worship of the Sungod: "Everyone now take a little rest to remove all fatigue and distress!"

pūjana sājana,   koro saba jana,
tāhāte suraja pūji
karpūra candana,   vividha pakkānna,
pāñca phule bhora sāji

"Everyone should help collecting the paraphernalia of the Sūrya pūjā—camphor, sandalwood pulp, different cooked dishes and five kinds of flowers."

devatā bhavane,   thākibe jatane,
loiyā āpana sakhī
pūjana lāgiyā,   jatana koriyā,
baṭure ānibe ḍāki

"Stay at the Sūrya-Mandira, taking Your girl-friends along, and carefully have a *brāhmaāa* called for the *pūjā*."

jaṭilā vacane,   saba sakhīgaṇe,
*   śayana korilā āsi*
rāire vākhāne,   saba sakhīgaṇe
*   śekhara vākhāne hāsi*

"All the *sakhīs* then went to take rest on Jaṭilā's order, while Rāya śekhara and all the *sakhīs* laugh at the jokes that Rāi makes." (50)

śrī rāga — tāla rūpaka

rādhikā rūpasī   loiyā tulasī
*   kohoye marama kathā;*
kānane gamana   koroho ekhona
*   nāgara śekhara yathā*

"Rādhikā Rūpasī (beautiful Rādhikā) took Tulasī along and told her from the heart: "Go now to the forest, where My king of lovers is!"

samaya bujhiyā   sarasa hoiyā
*   milibe nāgara kāna;*
catura nikaṭe   kohibe kapaṭe
*   rākhibe āpana māna*

"Understanding the time, be *rasika* and meet this Nagara Kāna. Go to this clever boy and tell Him false words, keeping your honour."

tulasī ulasī ,   monete haraṣi
*   colilā rāira bole;*
tāmbūla karpūra   loiyā phula-hāra
*   mililā sarasī kūle*

"Tulasī blissfully followed Rāi's order and went to the bank of Her lake, taking betelleaves with camphor and a flower garland with her."

> *dekhiyā tulasī   nāgara ulasi*
> *yatane bosāi kāche;*
> *āpana ākuli   kohilā sakali*
> *rāiyera gamana puche*

"Seeing Tulasī, Nāgara was very happy and attentively seated her close by. Then He anxiously told her how love-smitten He was and asked her if Rāi was coming."

> *e dhani caturi   nā koro cāturī*
> *āmāra śapati tore;*
> *rādhāra kuśala   kohiyā sakala*
> *śītala koroho more*

"O fortunate girl, I swear you, don't be clever with Me, but soothe Me by telling Me about Rādhā's welfare!"

> *se ye vinodinī   divasa rajanī*
> *antare khelaye mora;*
> *śutile svapane   dekhiye se'jane*
> *śapati koriye tora*

"This Vinodinī (pleasing girl) plays in My heart day and night. I swear you, I see Her in My dreams and when I sleep!"

> *samaya jāniyā,   śekhara āsiyā*
> *sumadhura kori bole*
> *se ye vinodinī   āsibe ekhoni*
> *thākoho sarasī kūle*

"Knowing the time has come, RāyaŚekhara came and sweetly said: "This Vinodinī Rāi will come now. Stay here and wait on the bank of Her *kuāḍa*." (51)

rāginī boḍāri — tāla eka tālā

tulasī caturā, kohoye madhurā,
 kātara dekhiyā kāna
tuṣiyā tāhāre, colilā ṣatvare,
 rākhiyā āpana māna

"Clever Tulasī spoke sweetly and, seeing how anxious Kṛṣṇa is, she consoled Him and then quickly went off, keeping her honour."

vīrā vṛndā āsi, rāira sarasī,
 sājāyalo nija mane
kori samāpana, āsite bhavana,
 tulasī mililā vane

"Vīra and Vṛndā came and decorated Rādhākuāḍa according to their liking. After finishing that they went home and met Tulasī in the forest."

hāsa parihāse, rāiko āoyāse,
 āilā sakala sakhī
śekhara sahite, vāratā śunite,
 sajala rādhāra āṅkhi

"All the *sakhīs* then came to Rāi's abode, laughing and joking. When Rādhā heard the news (about Kṛṣṇa's arrival at Rādhākuāḍa) along with Rāy Śekhara, Her eyes were filled with tears." (52)

❁

madhyāhna līlā
dhānaśī — tāla rūpaka

tulasī vacane, saba sakhīgaṇe,
 deva pūjibāra tare.
vidhi agocara, nānā upahāra,
 pūjā bhājana bhare

"On Tulasī's instigation all the *sakhīs (kiṅkarīs)* prepared the tray for the worship of the sun-god with many different ingredients, that are not perceived even by the Creator."

cini pheṇī kalā, mākhana rasālā,
 reuṛī kadamba tilā.
purī puyā khājā, peḍā sarabhājā,
 rādhikā koriyāchilā

"śrī Rādhikā had prepared sweets as Cini, Pheāī, Puyā (a kind of pancake), Khājā (sweets made with sugar and flour), Peḍā (milksweet) and savouries like bananas, butter, mangoes, rhubarb, Kadamba, sesame, Purīs and Sarabhājā (a sweet prepared by frying milk-film)."

amṛta kelikā, ādi se laḍḍukā,
 saghṛta mudga jhuri.
devatā pūjane, koriyā yatane
 bundi rasakarā khiri

"She carefully prepared Amṛta Keli-pies, *laḍḍus*, *dāl* with *ghī*, Bundi (pills of wheat dropped in *ghī*), Rasakarā (a sweet and juicy drop made of the kernel of coconut) and *kṣīra* (sweet rice) for the *pūjā* of the deity."

agora candana,   bharilo bhājana,
*   sugandhi phulera mālā*
atula amūla,   karpūra tāmbūla,
*   sājala sakala ḍālā*

"She filled Her basket with exquisite sandalpaste, fragrant flowergarlands and incomparibly valuable camphor-scented betelleaves."

saṅginī raṅgiṇī,   rūpa taraṅgiṇī,
*   bosiyā mandira mājhe*
madana mohana,   mohite yatane
*   korilā rāiko sāje*

"Accompanied by Her girlfriends, who are like rivers of beauty, She sat in Her abode. They ornamented Rāi in such a way that She could enchant even the enchanter of Cupid (Kṛṣṇa)."

sabāre satvara,   korilā śekhara,
*   dekhiyā uchara belā*
jaṭilā caraṇa,   koriyā vandana,
*   colilā sakala bālā*

"Kavi Rāy Śekhara prods everyone up to hurry, seeing that it is getting late. All the young girls then offered their obeisances to Jaṭilā's lotus feet and ran off." (53)

divābhisāra suraṭa sāraṇga

tapanaka tāpe,   tapata bhelo mahītala,
*   bālukā dahana samān*
coṛolo manorathe,   bhāvinī colu pathe,
*   tāpa tapana nāhi jān*

"The surface of the earth was scorched by the sunshine and the sand burned like fire. Still, Bhāvinī (emotional Rādhā) mounted the chariot of Her desires and ignored the solar heat."

hari hari premaka gati anivāra!
navīna yauvani dhani,   caraṇa kamala jini
tabahuṇ koyolo abhisāra

"Hari Hari! The course of love cannot be stopped! The feet of this young fortunate girl are softer than lotus flowers, but still She rushed out to meet Kṛṣṇa."

kula guṇa gaurava,   satī jaśa apajaśa,
tṛṇa kori nā mānaye rādhe
mana māhā madana,   mahodadhi uchalalo,
ḍubalo kula mariyāde

"Rādhā did not consider Her family's reputation, Her fame as a chaste girl or the infamy of the opposite to be more than a blade of grass. The great ocean of Cupid surged within Her mind and inundated Her family honour."

śata śata vighini,   jitalo anurāgiṇi,
sādhalo manamatha tantra
guru jana nayana,   nivārite suvadani
pāṭha koroye maṇi mantra

"Passionate Rādhā thus conquered hundreds of obstacles by using Cupid's *tantra* (magic amulet). To stop the eyes of Her superiors (from noticing) this fair-faced girl recited *mantras* and used magic gems."

keli kalāvati,   kusuma sarasi kule,
kauśale koyolo payān
joto chilo manoratha,   pūralo manamatha,
iha kavi śekhara gāna

"Thus the playful and artful Rāi cleverly arrived on the bank of Kusuma Sarovara. The poet Rāy śekhara sings: Cupid fulfilled all the desires on Her mental chariot." (54)

❁

śrī rādhār bhāvonmāda

hema yūthī varatati tamālera gāy
tāhā dekhi tarala āṅkhi vakra kori cāy
candramukhī ḍāki sakhi bole dekho ki
kānu kole bosi khele kon rājāra jhi
more dekhi pāṭābukī nā korilo ḍor
para puruṣe rasa variṣe chāṛite nāi tor
parera bole je jana bhole ki bolibo tāre
coṛi gāche bhrū-kuṭi nāce jiu hārābāra tāre
śekhara ruṣi kohe hāsi dhanī ageyāna
tamāla kole latā dole āne kohe āna

"When She saw this golden Yūthi-vine dangling around the body (trunk) of a Tamāla-tree Her restless eyes became crooked. Calling Her girlfriend Candramukhī, She said: "Sakhi, tell Me, what do you see? Which princess is there, playing on Kṛṣṇa's lap? When she sees Me, this shameless girl isn't even afraid! She cannot give up the shower of taste from another girl's man. What can I say to someone who is so engrossed in mistaking someone for someone else? Climb a tree and take her life by making your frowned eyebrows dance!" Rāya Śekhara laughs in

(loving) anger and says: Dhani is in ignorance. A vine dangles around a Tamāla-tree but She mistakes it for something else." (55)

śrī rādhār milanotkaāṭhā
rāgiāī bhāṭiyāri — tāla eka tālā

kānane kātara kulavatī rāi;
cakita nayāne ghana daśa diśa cāi
kokila kalarave vikala parāṇa;
guṇi guṇi bhāvinī bhelo nidāna
uśasi uśasi khasi khasi paḍu lora;
gada gada kaṇṭha śabada ghana ghora

"Chaste housewife Rādhā anxiously looked at the forest — with startled eyes She gazed in all ten directions. The singing of the cuckoos agitated Her heart and Bhāvini (emotional Rādhā) was dying at every breath. She breathed out deeply, tears of grief trickled from Her eyes and She made loud sounds with a faltering voice."

aichane āyali tapanaka geho;
pūjā upahāra tahi rākhilo keho
tahi paraṇāma kori baiṭhali dhanda;
sakhigaṇa kautuka koru nānā chanda
utapata tejato dīgha niśvāsa;
khene rodana koru khene koru hāsa
kohe kavi śekhara śuṇo sukumāri;
kāhe lāgi kātara milabo murāri

"In such a state She arrived at the Sūrya Mandira, where someone (a *mañjarī*) kept the paraphernalia of *pūjā* for later use. She offered obeisances to the Sungod and sat

down, while the *sakhīs* made different eloquent jokes. She breathed out deeply, sometimes weeping, sometimes crying and sometimes laughing. Kavi śekhara says: "Listen, Sukumārī! Why are You aggrieved? I will unite You with Murāri!" (56)

❀

śrī kṛṣāera utkaāṭhā
rāgiāī suhai — tāla daśakusi

kusumita kuñja hi kātara kāna;
kāminī lāgi koto koru anumāna
ki korobo koho more śubala sāṇgātī;
kalāvatī kāhe avadhi nāhi āti

"Kṛṣṇa anxiously sat in a flower-grove, wondering whether His ladylove would show up or not. "O Friend Subala, tell Me, what should I do? Why has Kalāvatī (the artful Rādhā) still not come?"

dāruṇa gurujana kiye koru bādhā;
kiye lāgi māninī bhoi gelo rādhā
tapanaka tāpe kiye coloi nā pāro;
guruyā nitamba pīna kuca-yuga bhāra

"Has Rādhā been stopped by Her cruel superiors, or is She angry with Me? Perhaps She found it too hot to go out today, or perhaps Her buttocks and Her two raised breasts are too heavy for Her to carry."

sva jana sahite kiye bāḍhalo leho;
ithe kiye dhani nāhi tejalo geho
vipada sampada kiye bujhai nā pāri;
kaichane vañcaye so sukumāri

bodhi śubala kohe śuno guṇavanta;
śekhara saha dhani milabo nitānta

"Perhaps this fortunate girl is exchanging affection with Her relatives, and therefore did not leave the house? I don't know what is good or bad anymore! How will I survive without this Sukumāri?" Subala, who was thus addressed by Kṛṣṇa, replied: "O qualified friend of mine, listen! This fortunate girl will meet with śekhara (Kṛṣṇa, the greatest of all)!" (57)

rāgiāī bhāṭiyāri — tāla eka tālā

vīrā vṛndā tathi,   āni rasavatī,
kānura nikaṭe yāy
mādhava mādhavī,   talāya bosiyā
dūrete dekhite pāya

"Vīrā and Vṛndā brought Rasavatī Rāi to Kṛṣṇa. From a distance they could see Mādhava sitting at the base of a Mādhavī-vine."

dekhi vīrā vṛndā,   subala sānandā,
e madhumaṅgala hāse
madana mohana,   pāolo cetana,
sukhera sāgare bhāse

"Seeing Vīrā and Vṛndā, Subala was in ecstasy and Madhumaṅgala laughed, while Madana Mohana regained consciousness and floated in an ocean of bliss."

doṇhāre loiyā,   ādara koriyā,
baiṭhāya āpana kāche

rāiyera kuśala,   kohoto sakala,
   sajala nayane puche

"Eagerly taking these two messengers along, Kṛṣṇa seated them close to Himself and asked them all about Rāi's welfare with tear-filled eyes."

vīrā kohe kāna,   koro avadhāna,
   ki pucho tāhāra tare
rāiyera svajana,   koriyā bhartsana,
   ruṣiyā rākhilo ghare

"Vīrā said: Listen, O Kān! What are You asking? Rāi was rebuked by Her superiors and angrily kept inside the house!"

śunite kāhinī,   ki hoilo nā jāni
   viṣāde nāgara ghora
vīrāra vadana,   nirakhi saghana,
   nayane bharalo lora

"Hearing this story, Nāgara became very morose, saying: 'Who knows what happened?' Staring at Vīrā's face He shed tears of gloom."

taba hi satvara,   āsiyā śekhara,
   kohoye nāgara rāje
ramaṇī mohana,   nā tole vadana,
   bāḍhalo adhika lāje

"Then Rāy śekhara quickly approached Nāgara Rāja and said: Ramaāī Mohana (Kṛṣṇa, the charmer of all the girls) did not lift His face. His embarrassment increased." (58)

❈

rāginī bhāṭiyāri — tāla eka tālā

vṛndā kohe kāna,   koro avadhāna,
   nāgarī sarasī kūle
devatā pūjane,   āninu yatane
   dekhoho bakula mūle

"**Vṛndā said: "Listen, O Kān! I have brought Nāgarī Rāi to the bank of Rādhākuāḍa on the pretext of Sūrya-pūjā. Look at the base of that Bakula tree!"**

hero dekho āra,   kuraṇga tomāra
   milalo raṇgiṇī saṇga
tāṇḍavī dekhiyā,   tāṇḍava chuṭalo,
   uṭhalo madana raṇga

cakora āsiyā,   cakorī milalo,
   sārikā milalo śuka
nāgara yāiyā,   nāgarī milaho
   ghucāo manera dukha

"**And look! Your deer is meeting with Raṇgiāī (Rādhikā's doe), and seeing Tāāḍavī (Rādhikā's peahen), Tāāḍava (Kṛṣṇa's pet peacock) comes running! Thus a wave of erotic pastimes surged! The Cakora bird came to meet the Cakorī and the śārikā met with the śuka. Now, O Nāgara, go to meet Your Nāgarī and eradicate Your sorrow!"**

vīrā vṛndā tathi,   koriyā yukati
   śubala maṇgale loiyā
kānana latāye,   lukāiyā rākhaye
   mādhava iṇgita pāiyā

"As Vīra and Vṛndā thus advised Him, Mādhava gave them a hint to take Subala and Madhumaṅgala into the vine-grove and keep them hidden there."

kāraṇa kohiyā, lukāi rākhiyā
kānana devatī yāy
mādhava mādhavī, milana dekhiyā
hāsaye śekhara rāya

"Explaining them why, the forest goddess (Vṛndā) went and kept them hidden. Rāya Śekhara laughs as he beholds the meeting of Mādhava and Mādhavī." (59)

madhu pāna
boḍāri — tāla eka tālā

duhuṇ mukha heraite duhuṇ bhelo dhanda;
rāi kohe tamāla mādhava kohe canda
cīta putali yeno rahu duhuṇ deha;
nā jāniye prema kemon achu neho
e sakhi dekho dekhi duhuṇka vicāra;
ṭhāmahi keho lakhai nāhi pāra

"When They beheld Each other's faces They became filled with doubt. Rāi said: "This is a Tamāla tree" and Mādhava said: "This is the moon." Their bodies were stunned like puppets. Who can understand Their *prema*? O *sakhi*! Look at the way They speculate about Each other, unable to recognise Each other's forms!"

dhani kohe kānanamoy dekhi śyāma;
so kiye guṇabo majhu pariṇāma
camaki camaki uṭhe nāgara kāna;

prati taru tale dekhe rāi samāna
doṇhe dohe jabahuṇ nicoya kori jāna;
duhuṇka hṛdaye paiṭhalo pāñca bāṇa

"Fortunate Rādhā said: "I see the whole forest as being filled with śyāma! Who knows what will ultimately become of Me?" Meanwhile Nāgara Kṛṣṇa's astonishment surged as He beheld Rāi at the base of each and every tree and vine. When They finally recognised Each other in a sure manner, Cupid, the wielder of five arrows, entered within Their hearts."

duhuṅ doṅhā milaho bāhu pasāri;
duhuṅ sukhe mātalo sab sukumārī
duhuṅ lei baiṭhalo bakulaka chāy;
aguru candana keho deya duhuṅgāya
duhuṅpada paṅkaje keho dei nīra;
keho keho vījai śītala samīra
madhumatī madhu loye korolo payāna;
kanaka beli bhori duhuṅkoru pāna
keho keho mochalo duhuṅ mukha canda;
lāje madana heri rahalahuṅ dhanda

"As the Divine Pair met Each other, They stretched out Their arms. All the tender *gopīs* were beside themselves of bliss when they saw how happy They were. They both sat down in the shade of a Bokula tree, while some *kiṇkarī* anointed Their bodies with sandalwood paste and *aguru*, some *kiṇkarīs* washed Their lotus feet with water and some fanned Them with a cool breeze. Madhumati then came with honey, filled a golden bowl with it and They both drank it, while some *kiṇkarīs* wiped Their moon-like faces. Seeing them, even Cupid became shy and bewildered."

duhu aṅge vikaśita vividha vikāra;
mātala manamatha lāja ki āra
duhuṅ meli baiṭhali nibhṛta nikuñje;
duhuṅ guṇa gāyato madhukara puñje
rādhā mādhava bhelo eka ṭhāy;
duhuṅmukha herato śekhara rāya

"Different ecstatic symptoms blossomed (appeared) on Their bodies. Cupid went mad, so was there any coyness left? The Divine Pair both sat down in a solitary grove, while the bumblebees sang Their glories. Rādhā and Mādhava were united— Rāya śekhara sees Their faces." (60)

hindola līlā
rāgiāī jayantī — eka tālā

kānana devati,   vṛndā satī tathi,
* rāiyera sarasī kūle*
vicitra jhulanā,   koriyā racanā,
* sukhada bakula mūle*

"The chaste forest goddess Vṛndā made a wonderful swing on the bank of Rādhākuāḍa at the base of a blissful Bokul-tree."

jhulanā upari,   nāgara nāgarī,
* āsiyā bosilā raṅge*
jhulāya jhulanā,   sakala lalanā,
* gada gada bhare aṅge*

"Nāgarī Rādhikā and Nāgara Kṛṣṇa blissfully sat down on the swing and all the *sakhīs* began to swing, Their bodies trembling of ecstasy."

jhulanā jhamake,   rādhikā camake,
* tā dekhi nāgara bhora*
hāsiyā hāsiyā,   bāhu pasāriyā,
* dhanire korolo kora*

"Nāgara was absorbed in seeing Rādhikā afraid of the forceful oscillation of the swing, so He smiled and stretched out His arms to take this fortunate girl on His lap."

rasavati loiyā,   kore āgoriyā,
* jhulaye rasika rāya*
sahacarī gaṇa,   jhulāya dviguṇa,
* susvare pañcama gāya*

"Taking Rasavatī Rāi on His lap, Rāsika Rāya (Kṛṣṇa) continued the swinging and the *mañjarīs* doubled the speed of the swinging, singing in the fifth note with fine voices."

jhulanā dhariyā,   madhura koriyā,
* kohoye śekhara rāy*
devatā pūjite,   jāibe turite,
* divasa bohiyā jāy*

"Holding the swing, Rāya Śekhara sweetly says: "Now quickly go to worship the *devatā* (the sun-god or Kṛṣṇa), for the day is floating by!" (61)

vaṁśī haraāa
rāgiāī dhānaśī— tāla eka tālā

jhulanā hoite,   nāmilā turite,
* gagane nirakhe belā*

> *phula tulibāre,   colila satvare,*
> *sakala ābhīra bālā*

"They looked at the sky to see what time it is, and quickly came off the swing. Then all the cowherd daughters hastily proceeded to pick flowers."

> *bhari phala phule,   śākhā sab lole,*
> *āsiyā paraśe mūla*
> *sakhī sab meli,   koriyā dhāmāli,*
> *tolaye vividha phula*

"The trees' branches were swaying from their heavy weight of fruits and flowers, that touched down to their roots. The *sakhīs* all met and began to pick different flowers, dropping them in their baskets."

> *sakala kānana,   maṇira bandhana,*
> *parāge pūrita bāṭa*
> *kori madhu pāna,   ali kore gāna,*
> *mayūra mayūrī nāṭa*

"The whole forest was studded with jewels and the paths were covered by flower-pollen. The bumblebees sang, drinking these flowers' honey, while the peacocks and peahens danced."

> *sugandhi karabī,   tolaye mādhavī,*
> *aśoka kiṁśuka javā*
> *e thala kamala,   tolaye sakala,*
> *dinamaṇi jini ābhā*

"The Vraja-girls picked a fragrant bouquet of Mādhavī-, Aśoka-, Kiṁśuka- and Javā-flowers, as well as all the land-lotuses, that shone brighter than the sun."

> *jāti yūthi,   tololo yuvatī,*
> *mallikā malatī cāmpā*
> *punnāga keśara,   tolaye nāgara,*
> *godalo vinoda jhāmpā*

"These young girls also picked Jāti-, Yūthi-, Mallikā-, Mālatī- and Campaka-flowers, while Nāgara-Kṛṣṇa picked Punnāga- and Keśara-flowers to make a blissful hair-decoration."

> *rasika nāgara,   guṇera sāgara,*
> *kusuma racanā kore*
> *hāsiyā hāsiyā,   āilā loiyā,*
> *rāire nikaṭe dhore*

"Rasika Nāgara, the ocean of attributes, smiled and picked flowers to bring them to Rāi."

> *bhuja-yuga tuli,   rāi suvadanī,*
> *tolaye lavaṅga phula*
> *rasika śekhara,   hoilā vibhora,*
> *dekhiyā bhujera mūla*

"Fair-faced Rāi lifted Her arms and picked Labaṅga-flowers, and Rāsika Śekhara (Kṛṣṇa) became absorbed in staring at Her armpit."

> *phula jhāmpā loiyā,   jatana koriyā,*
> *rāiko nikaṭe āsi*
> *dhanira āñcale,   dilena vibhole,*
> *phulera sahite vāṁśī*

"Taking a flower-*jhāmpā* (a girl's hair-ornament) in His hand, Kṛṣṇa carefully approached Rāi and placed it

in the hem of Her garment, accidentally placing His flute with the floral ornament."

> *pāiyā muralī,   rādhikā se beli,*
> *   rākhilā viśākhā pāśe*
> *viśākhā jatane,   korilā gopane,*
> *   śekhara dekhiyā hāse*

"Getting the flute, Rādhikā kept it in Viśākhā's care and Viśākhā carefully hid it. Seeing this, Rāy śekhara laughs." (62)

༝

> *vaṁśī sandhāna*
> *rāgiāī dhānaśī— tāla eka tālā*

> *sakhīgaṇa meli,   loiyā muralī,*
> *   colilā nibhṛta ghare*
> *nāgara śekhara ,   poḍolo phāṇphara,*
> *   muralī nāhiko kore*

"The *sakhīs* met and took the flute into a solitary abode, and Nāgara śekhara became perplexed, not having His flute in His hand."

> *lāje lājāyali,   nā dekhi muralī,*
> *   rāiyera vadana cāy*
> *rādhikā caturī,   koriyā cāturī,*
> *   sakhīra nikaṭe yāy*

"Embarrassed at not seeing His Muralī, Kṛṣṇa stared at Rāi's face, and clever Rāi went and joined Her *sakhīs*."

> *madana mohana,   pāiyā cetana,*
> *   suthira korolo cita*

> *muralī haraṇa,   rāiyera karaṇa,*
>   *gamane bujhalo rīta*

"Madana Mohana came back to His senses and became calm. Soon He understood that stealing His flute was Rāi's doing."

> *rāi rasavatī,   sakhīra saṁhati,*
>   *muralī korolo curi*
> *raṇga bāḍhāite,   śekhara gopate,*
>   *nāgare koholo ṭhāri*

"Rasavatī Rāi with Her assembled *sakhīs* thus stole the flute. Just to increase the fun, Rāy śekhara secretly gave a wink to Nāgara." (63)

❁

> *iṇgita bujhiyā,   nāgara āsiyā,*
>   *dhorilo rāiera kore*
> *se sab āṭapa,   sāṭapa dekhiyā,*
>   *rādhikā ḍorali ḍore*

"Understanding the hint, Nāgara came and held Rāi's hand. Seeing all this proud and shameless behaviour, Rādhikā became scared."

> *bhoye bhītā bālā,   gelo sab kalā,*
>   *mukhe nā niḥsore rā*
> *hiyā dulu dulu,   cāhe ḍhulu ḍhulu*
>   *āulāilo sab gā*

"This young girl got so scared that all Her cleverness disappeared and not a word came from Her mouth.

Her heart throbbed and She looked anxiously all around while Her whole body became agitated."

> *heriyā lakṣaṇa,　　nāgara tokhona,*
> *　dhanīre dhorilo cora*
> *māgaye muralī,　　ukaṭe kāñculi*
> *　madane hoiyā bhora*

"Seeing these signs, Nāgara held fortunate Rāi tightly. Overcome with lust He stuck His hand in Her blouse, looking for His flute."

> *dhanī kohe kān,　　koro avadhāna,*
> *　lalitā loilo baṁśī*
> *tomāre cañcala,　　dekhiyā sakala,*
> *　ramaṇī koroye hāsi*

"Fortunate Rādhā said: "Listen carefully, O Krṣṇa! Lalitā has taken Your flute. Seeing how restless and naughty You are, all the girls are laughing."

> *rāiyera vacane,　　colilā tokhone*
> *　madana mohana rāy*
> *lalitā jāniyā,　　kohoye ṭhāriyā,*
> *　muralī viśākhā ṭhāy*

"On Rāi's advice, Madana Mohana Rāy then went forwards to look for His flute on Lalitā, who told Him with a hint that Viśākhā had it."

> *lalitā vacana,　　bujhiyā tokhona,*
> *　viśākhā sāṭope bole*
> *tomāra murali,　　dekhiluṇ e beli,*
> *　campaka latāra kole*

"Understanding Lalitā's hints, Viśākhā proudly told Kṛṣṇa: 'I have seen Your Murali flute on Campakalatā's breasts."

śuniyā vacana, tarāse tokhona,
kohoye campakalatā
tuṇgavidyā pāśe, murali rākhiyā,
indulekhā gelo kothā

"Hearing these words, Campakalatā became scared and said: "I have seen Indulekhā keep the flute with Tuṇgavidyā— where has she gone?"

citrā camakitā, colilā turitā,
dekhiyā e sab raṇga
raṇgadevī pāśe, bosilā tarāse
sudevī tāhāra saṇga

"Citrā was amazed and quickly came to witness all this fun. Fearfully she sat next to Raṇgadevī in the company of Sudevī."

nāgara śekhara, nā pāi ṭhāhoro
sabhāre dhariyā bule
sakala jubati, koriyā jukati,
bosilā mādhavī mūle

"Nāgara śekhara could not ascertain (with whom the flute was) so He wandered around grabbing each *sakhī*. All the young girls then deliberated, sitting at the base of the Mādhavī tree."

hāsiyā lalitā, ruṣi kohe kothā
śuno he nāgara rāja

tarala bāṁśer, śukhāno kāṭha to
 tāhāte kāhāra kāja

"Lalitā laughed and said angrily: "Listen O king of playboys! Who needs this dry and light piece of bamboo flute of Yours anyway?"

phorā kāṭhi khāna, ki tāra vākhāna
 kohite nā bāso lāj?
māgiho āmāre dibo je tomāre,
 jadi vā thākaye kāj?

"Aren't You ashamed to be so attached to a lousy piece of perforated wood? You can ask me anything You need and I will give it to You."

tāhāra vacana, śuniyā tokhona,
 kohoye śekhara rāy
śunoho nāgara, nā hao kātara,
 murali dhanīra ṭhāy

"Hearing these words, Rāya Śekhara says: "Listen O Nāgara! Don't be upset! The flute is with Dhanī Rāi!" (64).

☙

rāgiāī paṭha mañjarī — tāla lophā

e dhani sundarī kohi puna toy;
deho muralī dhani rākhaho moy
jīvana avadhi dhani tuyā vaśa hām;
gāiye muralīte tuyā yaśa nāma
muralī vihane mora tanu bhelo bhār;
jītala manamathe muralīka tār
so guṇamaya vaṁśī kāhe lāgi gelo;
hā hā hatavidhi eto dukha delo

heraite kānuka iha anutāpa;
śaśimukhī hṛdaye haraṣe puna kāmpa
dhādhase dhari dhani nāgara pāṇi;
iṅgite śekhara vāṁśī dilo āni

"O beautiful and fortunate girl, I tell You again—save Me by returning My flute! I will be under Your control for as long as I live and I will sing Your name and fame with My flute!"

"Without My flute My body has become a heavy burden. Muralī's call defeated Cupid (My lusty desires)! Why has such a qualified flute gone? Alas, alas! My ill fate made Me unhappy!"

"When She saw Kṛṣṇa lamenting in this way, śaśimukhī (moon-faced Rādhā)'s heart throbbed of joy. Holding Nāgara's hand, Dhanī Rāi beckoned to Rāy śekhara to bring the flute." (65)

❁

rāgiāī suhai — tāla eka tālā

pāiyā vaṁśī,   nāgara hāsi,
bosi sabāra pāśe,
sakala bālā,   cāṇdera mālā,
mucaki mucaki hāse

"Getting His flute back, Nāgara smiled and sat down with all the other *gopīs*, that shone like a row of moons and were all smirking."

vana devati,   āsiyā tathi,
koilo anumāna
vadana śukhā,   dekhiyā bhukhā,
korāilo madhupāna

"Vṛndā, the forest goddess, came there and thought: "I see that Their faces are parched and They are thirsty (yearn for erotic happiness)", so she brought Them wine to drink."

> *hoiyā śītala,   kāme vikala,*
> *rādhā kānura mana*
> *bhāviyā mane,   sakhī sane,*
> *cāhe ghana ghana*

"Thinking: "Now Rādhā and Kānu have cooled off and Their minds have become agitated with lust", she stared at Them deeply with the *sakhīs*."

> *caturā sakhī,   doṇhāre rākhi,*
> *keli vilāsera ghare*
> *chalanā kori,   āilā sari,*
> *phula gāṇthibāra tare*

"The clever and wise *sakhīs* kept the Divine Pair within Their erotic play-house and went off on the pretext of picking flowers (leaving Them in peace)."

> *tabe jubatī,   nāgari tathi,*
> *nāgara kori kore*
> *madana dukhī,   śekhara sukhī,*
> *titila āṇkhira lore*

"Then the young heroine (Rādhā) sat down there and took Her hero on Her lap. Cupid was sad, but Rāya Śekhara was happy and tears trickled from his eyes." (66)

❀

sambhoga
rāgiāī dhānaśī — tāla eka tāla

nāgara nāgarī keli vilāsa;
heraite manamathe lāgalo tarāsa
vinodinī cumbai nāgara vayān;
madana mahodadhi bhari pāñca bāṇa
unamata manamatha gelo saba lāja;
nūpura kiṅkiṇī kaṅkaṇa bāja
vilasai mādhava mādhavī sāthe;
akhaṇḍa piyūṣa rasa nā poḍoye bādhe
śrama jala pūralo duhuṅ jana gāya;
vījana vījaye śekhara rāya

"Seeing Nāgara and Nāgarī's playful love-game, Cupid became alarmed. Vinodinī kissed Nāgara's face and the five arrows of Cupid filled up the ocean of eros. All shame went far away due to the erotic frenzy and Their anklebells and waistbells chimed in time. It was as if an unrelenting stream of nectar-juice was flowing from Mādhava and Mādhavī's pastimes. The bodies of the Divine Pair were filled with perspiration and Rāya śekhara fanned Them to cool Them off." (67)

❀

atha jala-krīḍā
rāgiāī baḍāri — tāla eka tālā

duhuṅ rasa rāśi	*samāpalo hāsi*
rati raṇa raṅge	*śrama bhelo aṅge*
gāṇthi phula mālā	*mile vrajabālā*
jala keli sādhe	*colu dhani rādhe*
yuvatī samāje	*śobhe yuvarāje*

sabhe eka tāne   kori koru gāne
sarasi salile   paiṭhe sa līle

"They laughed as They completed Their abundance of *rasa*. Their bodies were exhausted from the fun of the erotic battle. The girls of Vraja met after stringing flower garlands. Rādhā went to the bank of Her pond to accomplish Her water-sports. The beautiful prince (Kṛṣṇa) shone amidst the assembled young girls, who all sang a song in the same tune as He playfully entered into the water of Rādhākuāḍa."

kariṇīra saṇge,   kari-vara raṇge,
duhu duhu meli,   koru jala-keli
sakhī-gaṇa nipuṇā,   beḍhalo haṭhinā,
keho dei nīre,   keho loi cīre
keho dei tālī,   keho bole bhāli,
kānu mukha móḍi,   jala dei jori
keho keho hāri,   keho dei gāri,
keho bhāgi dūre,   camake nehāri

"That best of elephants sported with His she-elephants. They met and played in the water. The expert *sakhīs* rashly surrounded Kṛṣṇa. One splashed Him with water, another one took His clothes off, one clapped her hands, and another one said: 'Bravo!' Kānu turned His face away and violently splashed the *gopīs*. Some *gopīs* were defeated, some attacked, while some ran far away and looked on in amazement."

kānu kore beḍi,   dhayala kiśorī,
salila agādhā,   lei colu rādhā
hari-ka aṇke,   bhāsata saṇge,
pātala cīre,   bekata śarīre

> *nirakhite kāna,   hāne pāñca bāṇa,*
> *dhanī kori buke,   cumba dei mukhe*
> *dhanī kuca jora,   hāsi dei moḍā,*
> *hari puna sādhā,   ānali rādhā*

"Kiśorī Rādhā embraced Kānu and clasped Him. Hari took Her into the deep water, where She floated together with Him on His chest, Her bodily beauty revealed through Her thin clothes. When Kāna saw this He was struck by Cupid's arrows. Holding Dhani Rādhikā to His chest, He kissed Her on the mouth and grabbed Her breasts. Rādhikā then smiled and covered Her breasts." Hari then brought Rādhā back with some effort."

> *rākhali nīre,   alapahi dūre*
> *paduminī thāre,   calali vihāre*
> *kamalinī ṭhāme,   milali śyāme,*
> *sakhīgaṇa meli,   koru koto keli*
> *kori parihāse,   vividha vilāse*
> *sabhe uṭhe tīre,   parihari cīre*
> *nāgara saṇge,   koro rasa raṇge,*
> *kiye bhelo śobhā,   śekhara lobhā*

"Hari kept Rādhikā a little distance away from Himself and began to enjoy with the other lotus-like *gopīs* She kept on the shore, urging them also to come into the water. These lotus-like *sakhīs* then came and met śyāma in the water, where they played different pastimes with Him in a joking fashion. How beautiful they were when they played these *rasika* games with their Nāgara (amorous hero)! Rāya Śekhara is very eager to relish that beauty!" (68)

🪷

sūrya pūjā
rāgiāī bhāṭiyāri — tāla eka tālā

kusumita kuñja,   kalapa taru kānana,
maṇimaya maṇḍapa mājha
āilā kalāvati,   saba jana saṁhati,
kore loi pūjana sāja

"Kalāvati (Rādhā, the artful girl) took all Her friends and maidservants along to a jewelled altar in the middle of a flower-filled *kuñja* in a forest of wish-yielding trees, taking Her *pūjā*-paraphernalia with Her in Her hands."

kuṅkuma candana,   keśara anupama
campaka mālati māla
bahu vidha vana phula,   nīra suśītala
bahu upahāra rasāla

"There were many *rasika* paraphernalia— vermilion, sandalwood pulp, matchless saffron, garlands of Campaka- and Mālatī-flowers, many kinds of sylvan flowers and cold water."

bhānu bhavane dhari,   rākhalo sāri sāri
dadhi ghṛta ratana pradīp
sahacarī meli,   keli kalāvatī
baiṭhalo deva samīp

"Keli Kalāvatī (playful and artful Rādhā) also kept rows of jewelled lamps and pots with yoghurt and *ghī* in the solar temple. Then She and Her maidservants sat down near the deity."

111

nija rase bhāsi,　　hāsi dhani boloi,
　　śuno śuno kānana devī
deva pūjana vidhi,　　je jon jānaye
　　tāhe se ānaho sevi

"Floating in Her own *rasa*, Dhanī Rāi smiled and said: "Listen, listen O sylvan goddess (Vṛnde)! Bring someone here who knows the rules in worshipping this deity!"

rāiko carita,　　jāniya śekhara,
　　jāi milolo baṭu pāśe
vacana viśeṣe,　　lei madhumaṇgala
　　āoli deva āwāse

"Knowing Rāi's feelings and conduct, Rāya śekhara went to get a *brāhmaāa*. After persuading him to come with special arguments, he managed to bring Madhumaṇgala to the temple." (69)

✿

rāgiāī bhāṭiyāri — tāla eka tālā

tāre dekhi,　　mane sukhī,
　　elāye māthāra keśa
rasika nāgara,　　rasera sāgara,
　　dhorilo brāhmaṇera veśa

"Seeing this, Rasika Śekhara (Kṛṣṇa), who is an ocean of *rasa*, blissfully dishevelled His hair and dressed Himself like a *brāhmaāa*."

gole pāṭā,　　bhāle phoṇṭā,
　　kośā kośi kore

choṭa kāchā,　　　　　　moṭā koñcā,
　　　　kaṭi āṇṭi pore
loiyā puṇthi,　　　　　　hoiyā jati,
　　　　āilā devera ghare
pūjāra sajja,　　　　　　dekhi dvija,
　　　　mana san san kore

"Dressed as a *brahmacārī*, wearing a scarf around His neck, a dot on His forehead and Kuśa-grass in His hands, a short fold in (the back of) His *dhotī* and a large fold in the front, rings on His fingers and a book in the hands, Kṛṣṇa came to the temple. When He saw the *pūjā*-paraphernalia, this *brāhmaña* (Kṛṣṇa) became very happy."

nirakhi lāḍu,　　　　　　hariṣa baḍu,
　　　　kohe bāraṁbāra
āiso sabhe,　　　　　　pūjaho deve,
　　　　roite nāhi āra

"Seeing the *laḍḍus*, Madhumaṅgala was in ecstasy and repeatedly said: "Come on everybody! Worship this deity— nothing of this will be left!""

heri baṭu,　　　　　　kori cāṭu,
　　　　kohe sudhāmukhī
nāgara pāne,　　　　　　cāya saghane,
　　　　baṭu kaṭu dekhi

"Seeing this *brāhmaña*, Sudhāmukhī (nectar-faced Rāi) spoke flattering words to him. After looking harshly at Madhumaṅgala, She stared at Her Nāgara."

kori jatana,　　　　　dhari āsana,
　　　　baṭu bosāilā

rāira saṇgi,　　　raṇgera raṇgi,
modaka dekhāilā

"Diligently Rāi brought a seat and seated Her *brāhmaāa* (Kṛṣṇa) on it. Rāi's companion showed Kṛṣṇa, the enjoyer of fun-sports, the sweets."

asthira jāni,　　　vinodinī,
modaka dilā kore
āsana vasana,　　　bhūṣaṇa diyā,
baṭura varaṇa kore

"Knowing Him to be restless, Vinodinī placed the sweets in His hands. Then She accepted this *brāhmaāa* by offering Him a seat, garments and ornaments."

chanda dhari,　　　raṇga kori,
kohe kundalatā
bhānura kole,　　　kānu khele,
ei se bhalo kathā

"Insinuatingly and playfully, Kundalatā said: "Kānu plays on the lap of Bhānu (Vṛṣabhānu-nandinī Rāi). This is a good thing!"

naṣṭa loke,　　　duṣṭa kothā,
kohilo buṛira kāṇe
ruṣṭa hoiyā,　　　duṣṭa māgi,
āilā pūjāra sthāne

"Wicked people have gossiped in Jaṭilā's ear, and now she is angrily coming to the *pūjā*-place, wanting to make trouble."

sabhe meli,   kore keli,
bosi pūjāra ghare
dekhi buṛi,   śekhara sāṛi,
sabāra satvara kore

"Everyone was now playing, sitting in the *pūjā*-abode. Seeing Jaṭilā approaching, Rāya Śekhara is warning everyone." (70)

śrī rāga — tāla eka tālā

āyāna catura boṛo sadā māthā ṭhāṛ;
māyera sane,   āilā bone,
korite kathā doṛha

"Āyāna (Abhimanyu, Rādhā's would-be husband) is very clever and always keeps his head cool. Speaking harsh words, he came with his mother (Jaṭilā) into the forest."

hariṣa viṣāda,   bhālo manda
mane mane guṇe;
rāira rīti,   bujhite tathi,
bosilā maṇḍapa koṇe

"In a joyful and sorrowful mood he considered the good and bad of Rāi's behaviour. Understanding everything he sat down in a corner of the pavillion."

śaśuri āṛe,   jāni bhoye,
bhīta bhelo dhani
gāyera vasana,   khasaye saghana,
mukhe nā niḥsare vāṇī

"Casting sidelong glances at Her mother-in-law, Dhanī Rāi became afraid. Her garment dropped off Her body and She could not utter a word."

vipada ati,   bujhi tathi,
kohe sakala nārī
gopata kothā,   bekata hobe,
ebe kibā kori

"Understanding the danger, all the girls spoke amongst each other: "Our secrets will now become revealed. What shall we do now?"

rāi kātara,   ḍore vikala,
mone vicāra kore
duṣṭa mati,   dekhi pati,
nā jāni ki kore

"Greatly agitated by fear, Rāi thought to Herself: "I don't know what My husband will do when he sees what naughty things we are up to."

kohe baṭu,   hoiyā kaṭu,
brahmacārī śyāme
āyāna māye,   loiyā jāiye,
aiche koro kāme

"The *brāhmaāa brahmacārī* śyāma harshly said: "Will Abhimanyu's mother be able to take You away like this?"

kānu tokhon,   bhānu hoiyā,
phulera bhitora jāy
jokhon jemon,   tokhon temon,
bujhi kothā koy

"Kṛṣṇa then hid Himself within the flowers, becoming the sun (speaking like the deity) and spoke according to the circumstances."

śuno rādhā,   pativratā,
kene koro stuti
buṛir pāpe,   jālimu tāpe,
moribe tomāra pati

"Listen, O chaste Rādhe! Why are You praising Me? Your husband will die, and I will scorch Jaṭilā because of her sins!"

kolera kumāra,   sva jana joto,
gāi bhaiyiṣā āra
jhi jāmātā,   āni hetha,
korimu chāra khāra

"I will bring her lap's son, all her relatives, cows, buffaloes, her daughter and her son-in-law here and ruin them."

baṭu ati,   kore cāṭu,
bosi devera ghare
kare-joṛe,   veda poṛe,
deva mānābāra tare

"The *brāhmaāa* very humbly sat in the temple room, reciting the Veda with folded hands, honouring the Sun-god."

śuno deva,   dinamaṇi,
tomāy āmi jāni
stuti pāṭhe,   golā phāṭe,
śuno mora vāṇī

"Hear me, O god, O jewel of the day (the sun)! I know you! Listen to My words and My recital of prayers, that makes My voice burst!"

ei rādhā,   tori sadā,
bhoye bhelo bhora
dayā kori,   rākho nārī,
ei minati mora

"This Rādhā is always filled with fear of you, so please save this woman— this is My humble prayer!"

kundalatā,   dhani tathā,
kohe binoya vāṇī
rādhāra tore, hiyā jhure,
śuno dinamaṇi
bhoye dhani, hoiyā khini,
gole vasana diyā
deva nikaṭe,   niṣkapaṭe,
rohe dāṛāiyā

"Blessed Kundalatā then humbly said: "Hear me, O Dinamaāi (sungod)—I know that this Rādhā pleases your heart— now She is emaciated of fear. She always sincerely stands by you, O god, keeping Her cloth to Her neck (expression of humility)."

śekhara āge,   bor māge,
śuno divākara
se nā buṛi,   moruk puṛi,
rākho rādhāra ghara

"Rāya Śekhara first asks a boon, saying: "Hear me, O Divākara (sun)! May this old hag (Jaṭilā) scorch to death, but save Rādhā's house!" (71)

❀

śrī rāga— tāla daśakusi

karajoṛe kohe dhani,   śuno deva dinamaṇi,
janama sevana koinu tora
dhana jana parivāra,   sab jābe chāra khāra,
ei se kapāle chilo mora

"With folded hands Dhanī Rāi said: "Hear Me, O *deva* Dinamaāi! I have served you throughout My life! If My wealth, friends and relatives all perish, then that was written on My forehead (it was My fate)!"

dinamaṇi koro avadhāna!
pati jadi mori jābe,   tabe mora kibā hobe,
kon kāje rākhibo parāṇa?

"O Dinamaāi, hear me carefully! If My husband dies, then what will become of Me? How will I remain alive?"

devara nanada morā,   bāse jeno āṅkhira tārā,
śāśuri sohāga kore sadā
e sab moriyā jābe,   tabe mora kibā hobe
e tāpe kemone jīve rādhā

"My brother-in-law and My sister-in-law reside in the pupils of My eyes and My mother-in-law always treats Me with great love. If they would all die, then what would become of Me? How will this Rādhā survive all this afflic-tion?"

viṣāda viṣaṇṇa mon,   ḍāke sati nārāyaṇ,
baṭu cāṭu kore tāra pāśe

rādhāra vadana dekhi,　　　vikala hoiyā āṅkhi,
　　vikaṭa kapaṭa deva hāse

"In great sorrow and lamentation this chaste girl called upon Lord Nārāyāa, and the *brāhmaa* also anxiously prayed to Him, standing by Her side. Beholding Rādhā's face, the frightening deity smiled falsely, his eyes becoming agitated."

rāiyera binoy śuni,　　　kohe deva dinamaṇi,
　　prasanna hoinu tora tore
dhane jane pūrṇā hoiyā,　　　thāko satī pati loiyā
　　āpada nahibe tora ghore

"Hearing Rāi's humble submission, the solar god Dinamaāi told Her: 'O chaste girl! I am pleased with You. No calamity will strike Your home! Stay there happily with Your husband, friends and wealth!'"

deva dayāmoy dekhi,　　　ānande hoilā sukhī,
　　śuni boise āsana bhiṛiyā
nāgara mohinī dhanī,　　　pūje deva dinamaṇi,
　　baṭu deya sumantra poṛiyā

"Seeing the deity in a benign mood, Nāgara Kṛṣṇa's enchantress Dhanī Rāi became ecstatic and sat on Her seat to offer *pūjā* to the jewel of the day, while Her accompanying *brāhmaa* recited the proper *mantras*."

dhūpa dīpa gandha mālā,　　　diyā deva pūje bālā
　　āra koto śata upahār
baṭu sukhe mantra poṛe,　　　saghane huṅkāra chāṛe
　　dekhi buṛir hoilo camatkār

"This young girl then worshipped the sungod with hundreds of items, like incense, lamps, scents and garlands. Her *brāhmaāa* blissfully chanted the *mantras*, occasionally uttering loud roars. Seeing this, Jaṭilā was astonished."

> *nānā upahāre dhani, pūjā koilā dinamaṇi,*
> *avaśeṣe māge eka bor*
> *jadi hoilā anukūl, poṛuk māthāra phul,*
> *tabe se ghucaye sab ḍor*

"Blessed Rāi performed the Sūrya-pūjā with different paraphernalia and finally She begged for one boon: If you are favorably disposed towards Me, then let a flower fall from your head— then all My fear will be gone."

> *hāsi deva māthā nāṛe, jhara jhara phul poṛe,*
> *hulāhulī dei nāri-gaṇe*
> *dekhiyā devera mukh, bāṛaye sabhāra sukh,*
> *āśīṣ māgaye jane jane*

"The deity smiled and shook his head, causing flowers to shower from it. The women uttered *hulāhuli* (a female cry of joy) and everyone's bliss increased when they beheld the deity's face. Each person then began to ask the deity for benedictions."

> *sabār śire diyā hāt, baṭu kore āśīrbād,*
> *janama āiyati hoiyā thāk*
> *ei deva nirañjana, pūruk sabāra mana,*
> *naivedya prasād kichu cākh*

"'Placing his hand on eveyone's head, the *brāhmaāa* blessed everyone: "May you be with your husbands throughout your lives! May this stainless Lord fulfill everyone's desires and relish the offered foodstuffs."

> *vasane bāndhiyā sab,　　na rākhilo eke lab,*
> *loiyā colilā āra bone*
> *hiyāy boro hoilo ḍor,　　kāṁpe buṛi thara thara,*
> *āyān āsān pāilo mone*

"He tied everything in His cloth and did not leave anything at all. He took it all into the forest. Jaṭilā was very frightened at heart and began to tremble, but Abhimanyu felt relieved."

> *putere loiyā buṛi,　　palāilo guṛi guṛi*
> *patha vipatha nāhi māne*
> *ulaṭi pālṭi cāy,　　vasana nā rohe gāy,*
> *āyān bharasā kore mone*

"Old Jaṭilā took her son along and they walked off very slowly, not considering any dangers on the road. Abhimanyu felt so relieved that his eyes rolled about and his garments did not remain on his body."

> *doṇhe āsi boise ghore,　　rāire se praśaṁsā kore,*
> *māthāy āghāt sadā kore*
> *niṣedha korilo māy,　　ekathā nā koho kāy*
> *ghare aile mānāio sabāre*

"Both Abhimanyu and Jaṭilā returned home, praising Rāi and constantly hitting their heads with their hands. Abhimanyu forbade his mother: "Don't tell this event to anyone. When Rādhā returns home everyone should praise Her.""

hāsiyā śekhara koy,   āra kichu nāhi bhoy
more sabe koro paratīt
vilāsa mandire colo,   kautuke pāśaka khelo,
sakale suthira koro cīt

"**Rāya Śekhara laughs and says: "There is no need to fear anymore. Everyone believe me. Go to the *vilāsa nikuñja* and play there in ecstasy. No one need be afraid."**
(72)

❀

pāśa-krīḍāy paāa-nirdeśa

bhānu bhavane kori bahu vidha raṅga;
nāgara nāgarī jāy sakhīgaṇa saṅga
marakata maṇi ghare sukhada āsane;
pāśāy āsak hoïyā bosilā jatane
rāi kānu beṛiyā bosilā sakhīgaṇe;
atula rasera hāṭ pātilo madane
nāgara kohoye rāi śunoho vacan;
jadi vā khelibe pāśā āge koro paṇ

"**After having a lot of fun in the temple of the sun god, Nāgara Kṛṣṇa and Nāgarī Rādhā, along with Their girlfriends, proceeded to an emerald abode where there were blissful seats. Addicted to the game of Pāśā, Rāi-Kanu sat down, surrounded by Their girlfriends, and Cupid extended a matchless marketplace of *rasa*. Nāgara Kṛṣṇa said: "Rāi! Listen to My words! If You want to play Pāśā, then You place a wager first!"**

ei se khelāra rīti sudhāho sabhāre;
tumi āmi nahi ihā vidita saṁsāre
dhani bole koro paṇ tomāra muralī;
āmāra hoilo paṇ golāra hāṇsulī
kānu bole kibā paṇ korilā vinodini;

khelāra emon paṇ kabhu nāhi śuni
pāśaka khelāra paṇ śuno rasavatī;
śateka cumbana dāna ihāra uciti

"Now inquire about the rules of the game from everyone. You and I do not know this in this world." Dhanī Rāi said: "Place Your Muralī-flute as a stake. My wager will be the Hāṅsulī (crescent) necklace around My neck." Kṛṣṇa said: "O Vinodini, what kind of wager is this? I never heard of such a wager in a game! O Rasavati! Listen to this wager for the Pāśaka-game— You should place a hundred kisses at stake instead!"

mo jadi hāriye paṇ āge dibo tore;
tumi to hārile dibe ei se vicāre
paṇ śuniyā rādhā kohe bāre bār;
je khelibe khelun mui nā khelibo ār
kundalatā kohe dhani nā khelibe kene;
uttama hoilo paṇ khelo dui jane
lalitā kohoye kānu koro avadhān;
hārile cumbibe tumi bhṛngīra boyān

"If I lose I will first give You My wager and if You lose You will give Me Yours." Hearing of this wager, Rādhā said again and again: "Anyone who wants to play such a game can play it — I won't play anymore!" Kundalatā said: "Dhani, why don't You play anymore? This is the best wager You can imagine— play, both of You!" Lalitā said: "Kṛṣṇa, listen carefully! If You lose You must kiss the face of Bhṛṅgī (an aboriginal girl)!"

rādhikā hārile dibe gaja moti hār;
nahe vā āmrā tāhe koribo bicār
lalitār kothāy hāsiyā rasavatī
; khelāy vinoda pāśā nāgara saṇgati

pāṭīr upore sāri pātilo viśākhā;
dharilo pāśār pāṭī sundarī rādhikā
kohe kavi śekhara śuno sakhīgaṇ;
jay parājay dekho hoiyā mahājan

"When Rādhikā loses She will hand over Her thick pearl necklace, and otherwise we'll think of an alternative." When Rasavatī Rāi heard Lalitā's words She laughed. Nāgara should be able to enjoy this dice game. Viśākhā placed all the pieces of the game in a row and Sundarī Rādhikā held the row of Pāśas (dice stones). Kavi śekhara says: "Listen, O *sakhīs*! Become great and fair judges while watching who wins and who loses!" (73)

pāśā krīḍā
rāgiāī dhānaśī — tāla eka tālā

kara joṛi mantra poṛi rāi phele pāṭi;
poṛilo sarasa dāna cālāilo guṭi
sāṭopa koriyā dāna phelilo nāgara;
poṛilo nirasa dāna hoilo phāṇpara

"Rāi folded Her hands, recited *mantras* and threw a good score after due calculation. After that She moved Her pieces. Nāgara proudly threw His score, but He became perplexed when He saw how meagerly He scored."

rāi uṭhāiyā pāṭi phele āra bāra;
jininu jininu boli bole bāra bāra
ruṣiyā phelilo pāṭi rasika sujāna;
je dāna phelite cāhe nā poṛe se dāna

"Rāi threw again after calculation and repeatedly exclaimed: "I will win! I will win!" Rasika Sujana (Kṛṣṇa) angrily threw again, but did not score as much as He wished."

supāṭa nā poṛe pāṭi nā cāloye sāri;
viśākhā hāsiyā kohe nāgarera hāri
kalarava chala kori pāṭi loiyā kore;
haṭhe śaṭha phele dāna jinibāra tare

"After failing to score nicely Kṛṣṇa did not bother even to move His piece. Viśākhā laughed and said: Nāgara is defeated!" Through some tricky noise Nāgara took His piece away in His hand and threw another false score in order to still win."

taba huṅ poṛolo dāna kupaṭa tāhāra
dhani kohe mukhe lāja nāhiko tomāra
kuṅdalatā kohe dhani koro avadhāna
bhṛṅgīra adhara rasa kānu koru pāna

"Then He scored badly again and Dhanī Rāi told Him: 'Don't You have any shame at all?' Kundalatā said: "Dhani, beware! Let Kṛṣṇa drink the juice of Bhṛṅgī's lips!""

lalitā viśākhā kohe śuno kundalatā;
priya jane heno koho anucita kothā
khelilo vinoda khelā saṅge sakhīgaṇa;
śekhara loiyā jāy vinoda bhavana

"Lalitā and Viśākhā said: "Listen, O Kundalatā! It is improper to speak like that to your dear ones!" Thus Kṛṣṇa performed blissful pastimes with His *sakhīs*. Then Rāya Śekhara took them along to the abode of bliss." (74)

vana bhojana
rāgiāī baḍāri — tāla daśa kusi

govardhana girivara,   nikaṭahi maṇighara,
sukhada śitala manohara
kalapa tarura vana,   śobhiyāche vilakṣaṇa
samīpe rādhāra sarovara

"Close to Girirāja Govardhana is a jewelled abode, which is delightful, cool and enchanting. There is a specially beautiful forest of wish-yielding trees there, close to Rādhākuāḍa."

praphulla kamala tāya,   bhramarā bhramarī gāya,
cakravāka kore krīḍā-raṇa
madana dhanuka kore,   sadāi tāhāte phire,
jatane rākhaye sei vana

"Male and female bumblebees sing around the blossoming lotus flowers and Cakravāka-flamingos playfully fight there. Cupid always wanders around there, carefully protecting this forest with his bow and arrows."

avasara jāni khelā,   vṛndāra hoilo melā,
phula tuli ānilo satvara
uttama saṁskāra kori,   soṇāra thālite bhori,
sāri sāri piṇḍā thare thara

"Knowing which pastime was about to take place, Vṛndā came there and quickly began to pick flowers. She made the best arrangements, filling up golden trays (and placing them) in rows on the altar."

kori mone anumān, racilo bhojana sthān,
* āge āsan bosibāra tare*
sugandhi śītala jal, kori ati sunirmal
* jhara jhari bhori bhori dhare*

"After due consideration she first made seats for Them before making an eating-place. Then she poured out streams of cold, spotless and fragrant water."

āra joto upahāra, kori sab sambhāra,
* vṛndā sānanda hoiyā mane*
sakhīgaṇa nānā raṇge, nāgara nāgarī saṇge,
* praveśilā vilāsa bhavane*

"Vṛndā then blissfully collected all other ingredients (for Rādhā and Kṛṣṇa's enjoyment), and the *sakhīs* took Nāgara and Nāgarī, Who were playing different games, into that abode."

dekhiyā vṛndāra rīta, sabe bhelo ānandita,
* rasarāja bosilā bhojane*
mukhāni pākhāli nīre, mochalo pātala cīre
* vanadevī koroye sevane*

"Seeing Vṛndā's arrangements, everyone became very happy and Rasarāja (Kṛṣṇa) sat down to eat. Vanadevī Vṛndā then served Him by washing His face with water and wiping it with a thin towel."

eke eke upahār, bhuñje kānu bāre bār,
* rādhikā dekhiyā bhelo sukhī*
avaśeṣa piye jala, tabe bhuñje banaphol,
* jatane khāwāy sudhāmukhī*

"Kṛṣṇa enjoyed one preparation after the other, and when He saw Rādhikā He became happy. Finally He drank water and ate forest-fruits that Sudhāmukhī (nectar-faced Rādhā) fed Him."

śekhara satvara hoiyā,   āilo ḍābara loiyā
    ācamana korābāra āse
vilāsa mandira mājhe,   racilo pālaṇka śeje,
    tāmbūla sampuṭa tāra pāse

"Rāya Śekhara then quickly brought a bowl, wanting to wash Kṛṣṇa's mouth. Then he proceeded to make a love-bed in the love-cottage and placed a *pān*-box next to it." (75)

❀

rāgiṇī sāraṅga — tāla lophā

kuñje sundara śyāmara canda;
bahu vidha bhojana koroye ānanda
ācamana kori tāhe nāgara rāja;
rasabhare baiṭhalo kuñjaka mājha

"In the *kuñja* beautiful śyāma-cāṇd blissfully enjoyed so many different kinds of food. After flushing His mouth Nāgara Rāja sat down in the *kuñja* in great *rasika* bliss."

sukhada śejopari baiṭhalo kāna;
dhani avaśeṣa koru bhojana pāna
sahacarīgaṇa-meli bhuñjali rādhe;
ācamana kori colu śayanaka sādhe

"Kṛṣṇa sat down on the blissful bed while Dhanī Rādhā ate and drank His remnants with Her maidservants

and girlfriends. After that She flushed Her mouth and reclined."

rasamayī baiṭhali rasamaya pāś;
duhuṇ heri sakhīgaṇa koru parihās
vraja-ramaṇīgaṇa caturī sujāna;
karpūra tāmbūla dei pūralo boyān

"Rasavatī Rāi sat down next to Rasamaya śyāma. Seeing Them together, the *sakhīs* joked about Them. The Vraja-*gopīs* are very clever— they filled the mouths of the Divine Pair with camphor-laced betelnuts."

duhuṅ aṅge śubekata madana vikār;
sahacarīgaṇa heri bhelo bāhār
duhuṅ meli śutalo alasa gāy;
duhuṅ pada sevaye śekhara rāy

"Erotic transformations were clearly manifest on Their bodies. When the *sakhīs* saw this they went out of the *kuñja*. The two met and then reclined, Their bodies exhausted, while Rāya Śekhara served Their lotus feet." (76)

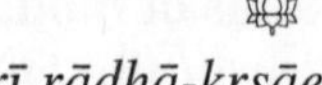

śrī rādhā-kṛṣāer nidrā līlā
āśāvarī — tāla eka tālā

kusumita kuñje alikula guñje
malaya samire bohe dhīre dhīre
rasavati saṅge rasamaya raṅge
dhani kori buke śutali sukhe

"In the flowering *kuñja* the bumblebees buzzed and the Malayan breeze blew gently as Rasavatī Rāi enjoyed pastimes with Rasamaya Kṛṣṇa. Taking Dhanī Rāi to His chest, Kṛṣṇa blissfully reclined."

dhari kuca kalase; ghumalo alase
kiśorī kiśora; niṇde bhelo bhora
rahali āveśe; dhani bhelo śeṣe
kānana devi; kokila sevi
korāyali gāne; jāgalo kāne
dhani uṭhi baiṭhe; kacāloi diṭhe

"Holding Her jug-like breasts, He fell asleep in exhaustion. Thus Kiśorī and Kiśora fell deeply asleep. Finally Dhani Rāi went into an *āveśa* (ecstatic absorption). The forest goddess arranged for cuckoos to serve Kṛṣṇa by waking Him up with their songs. Dhanī Rāi woke up and sat up, casting glances at Kṛṣṇa."

śekhara ṭhāri; loi jala-jhāri
duhuṇ mukha-cāṇde; dhoyāi suchāṇde
pān karpūre; duhuṇ mukha pūre

"Rāy Śekhara then took a jug of water and washed Their moon-like faces; then he filled Their mouths with camphor-laced *pān*." (77)

surata līlā

kusumita kānana kuñja kuṭīre;
tahi rasa vilasai kānu madhure
dhani kara dhari taba boloto kān;
sundari deho more surati dān

āju mana mānasa pūrāho mora;
adhara sudhā rasa pībau tora
tuyā kuca kalasa paraśa bhelo sādh;
nā koroho sundari iha sukhavād

"**Kṛṣṇa enjoyed sweet and tasty pastimes in a *kuñja kuṭīr* in a flower-garden. Holding Dhani Rāi's hand He said: "O Sundari, give Me the treasure of eros! Please fulfill My mind's desires today and let Me drink the nectar juice from Your lips. I want to touch Your pitcher-like breasts—O Sundari! Don't deprive Me of this happiness."**

so bihi mohe rākhabo joto din;
hām bhelo kevala tuhāri adhīn
ithe jab hām kabahuṇ kori ān;
tathi lāgi madhyata roholo pāṇca bāṇ
anunaya koroi kohoi lahu bāt;
dhani koro lei dha-ali nija māth
hāsi kohoi tahi rasavatī nārī;
śekhara kohe tuyā jāo bolihāri

"**Fate has kept Me dependent on You alone. If I ever act otherwise Cupid remains a mediator[2]." Thus He humbly spoke soft words, taking Dhani's hand and placing it on His own head. Rasavatī Rāi then smiled and spoke to Him, while Rāya Śekhara says: "All glories to You." (78)**

śrī rādhāra cāturī

majhu kara choṛaho nāgara kān;
ko jāne koichana suratika dān
hām abalā tāhe mati ati hīnā;
hām kāhā pāabo dān dachinā

suratika mūruti kabahuṇ nā dekhi;
sakhīgaṇe puchabo iha kori sākhi

(Śrī Rādhā tells Śrī Kṛṣṇa:) "O Nāgara! Let go of My hand! Who knows what the gift of eros is like? I am just a very simple girl— where will I get the wealth for such a gift? I have never seen the form of Cupid yet; ask My girlfriends— I call them as witnesses!"

jab hāme mīlabo śuno vara kān;
tab tohe de-abo suratika dān
kabahuṇ nā śunalo suratika nām;
āju tuhuṇ mohe koholi anupām
kāhe minati koru rāja kumār;
surati ki āchaye sātha hāmār
kohe kavi śekhara śunoho murāri;
surati nā jānaye bhānu kumāri

"Listen, O greatest Kṛṣṇa! When I meet You I will give You the treasure of eros. Never before have I heard the name of that matchless Cupid that You have spoken to Me now. O Prince, whence those humble petitions? Do I have that treasure of eros on Me perhaps?" Kavi śekhara says: "Listen, O Murāri! This daughter of Vṛṣabhānu knows nothing of love!" (79)

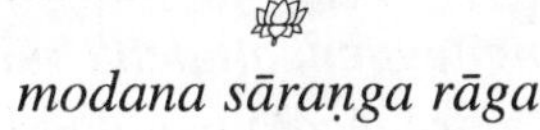

modana sāraṇga rāga

hāsi ḍhīṭ hari dhani kori kora;
pīboi adhara sudhā rasa bhor
cumbana beri vadana pālṭāi;
vasana dei ghana ghana lapaṭāi
kuca yuga kañcuka toḍoite kān;
dhani bhuje jāti rohoi sābdhān

tab nibi bandhe sughara dei hāth;
kākuti kori dhani dibo dei māth
nāgarī bodhaye nāgara kān
śekhara se beli rahu sābdhān

"Bold Hari laughed, held Dhani's hand and became absorbed in drinking the nectar of Her lips. She, however, obstructed His kisses and turned away Her face, covering it thickly with Her veil. Kṛṣṇa then began to tear at Her blouse to get at Her two breasts, but Dhani stopped Him with Her arms. Then He expertly placed His hands on Her girdle and Dhanī anxiously pleaded to Him (to stop). Nāgara Kān then addressed Nāgari Rāi, while Rāy Śekhara said: "Stay on guard!" (80)

modana

e dhani haṭhini kaṭhini tuyā cīta;
iha sab nā hoy nāgarī rīt
karo joṛi sundari māgoṇ parihār;
madana vedana dukha sohoi nā pār
eka beri rākhoho deho jīu dāna;
ājanama tuyā guṇa korobohu gān
haṭha chori bāhu bhiṛi deho dhani kor;
tuyā pāye soṇpaluṇ iha tanu mor
iṅgite anumati deali rāi;
kuṭila dṛgañcala madana jāgāi
nāgara nāgarī rasa avagāy;
dūre rohi dekhoi śekhara rāy

"O Dhani, You are so obstructive and Your heart is so harsh! This is not at all the behaviour of an amorous heroine! With folded hands I pray to You, O Sundari— I can no longer tolerate the pain of lust! Save My life this time and I will sing Your glories for as long as I live! Give up Your obstruction and embrace Me with Your arms— I have surrendered My body at Your feet!" Rāi then gave a hint of consent, awakening Cupid with Her askance glances. Thus Nāgara Kṛṣṇa and Nāgarī Rādhā immersed Themselves in *rasa* and Rāya śekhara witnesses it all from a distance." (81)

sankṣipta vilāpa
sāraṇga rāga

haraṣi bharasi hari dhari dhani buke;
rasamaya cumboi rasamayī mukhe
kamalinī kucayuga kamaṭha kaṭhore;
kānu kaṭhin kori dharoloi jore
adhare daśana cihna dei bāre bār;
camaki uṭhaye rāmā kori śītkār
kuca para deyalo nakhara āṇcare;
vasana bhūṣaṇa sab gelohi dūre

"Blissfully Hari kept Dhanī on His chest (in reverse pastimes) and Rasamaya śyāma kissed Rasamayī Rāi on the mouth. Kṛṣṇa kept His hard hands on the breasts of Kamalinī Rāi, that were as hard as turtle-shells. He made marks on Her lips with His teeth time and again and as Rāi became astonished She began to scream. Hari scratched Her breasts with His nails and removed all Her clothes and ornaments."

prati aṇge cumboi nāhiko vicāra;
madana mohana luṭe madana bhāṇḍāra
surata taraṇginī raṇginī rāi;
śyāma mātaṇga tahi avagāi

duhuṅ adharāmṛta duhuṅ mukhe pūre;
ab sab śekhara herai dūre

"Madana Mohana looted the storehouse of Madana (Cupid), kissing each of Rādhikā's limbs without distinction. Raṅginī (playful) Rāi is like a Gaṅgā-river of eros (or like a girl who rejoices in eros) in which the śyāma-elephant went to take a bath. They filled Their mouths with Each other's lip-nectar and RāŚekhara now witnesses this from a distance." (82)

eṛo eṛo mādhava tohe parihāra;
saghane talape jīu sohoi nā pāro
hām nava nāyarī śunoho mādhāi;
svāmī paraśa rasa kabahu nā pāi
ithe ati viparīta bhelohi mora;
strī vadha pātake bhoy nāhi tora

"Give up Your efforts, O Mādhava— I cannot tolerate the intense life on this bed anymore! Hear Me, O Mādhava! I am a young girl who has never tasted the touch of Her husband yet! Now everything is going against Me— You are not afraid even of the sin of murdering a woman!"

adhare daśana cihna kāhi deho dāruṇā;
mora jīu nikasai tora nāhi karuṇā
gadagada śabade kohoi dhanī boli;
mucaki hāsi hari samādhai keli
śrama jale pūralo duhuṅ keri gā;
śekhara jāi koru śītala bā

"Why are You making such deep cuts in My lips with Your teeth? My life is almost leaving Me— You have no mercy at all!" Dhani Rāi spoke with stuttering voice, while Hari just smirked and ended His love-making. Their bodies were studded with sweat drops and Rāy śekhara cooled Them off by fanning Them." (83)

śrī rādhā-kṛṣāera śayotthāna evaṁ vilāsa lakṣaāa gopana
rāga —sāraṇga

> *vilāsa sambari,　　　nāgara nāgarī,*
> 　　*bosilā kusuma śeje*
> *śramete ākula,　　　khosolo dukula,*
> 　　*kiśorī bikala lāje*

"After They had ended Their love game, Nāgara Kṛṣṇa and Nāgarī Rādhā sat down on Their bed of flowers. They were exhausted and Their garments had fallen off. Kiśorī Rāi was very embarrassed."

> *vilāsa mandire,　　　gavākṣa duyāre*
> 　　*rohiyā sakala sakhī*
> *monera ullāse,　　　dekhiyā vilāse*
> 　　*śītala hoilo āṅkhi*

"All the *sakhīs (mañjarīs)* stood at the windows of the temple of love-play and blissfully soothed their eyes by witnessing these pastimes."

> *dekhi avasare,　　　sakhinī satvare*
> 　　*paśilā vilāsa ghare*
> *doṇhāre loiyā,　　　jatana koriyā,*
> 　　*charama korolo dūre*

"Seeing their time to serve had come, the *sakhīs* and *mañjarīs* quickly entered into the temple of love and carefully removed the fatigue of the Divine Pair."

suśīlā sundarī,　　　　　nīre pūri jhāri,
*　　deolo doṇhāre kore*
uṭhiyā du jana,　　　　　pākhāli vadana,
*　　vasana bhūṣaṇa pore*

"Well behaved beautiful girls filled pitchers with water and poured it over the hands of the Divine Couple, who then got up, washed Their faces and put Their dresses and ornaments back on."

pālaṇka hoite,　　　　　bosilā sukhete,
*　　sukhada āsana pori*
vilāsa lakṣaṇa,　　　　　korolo gopana,
*　　śekhara jatana kori*

"They blissfully came off the bed and sat down on a delightful seat, after which Rāya Śekhara did his best to conceal the signs of Their lovemaking." (84)

❦

mañjarī ratana,　　　　　ānalo candana,
*　　lepalo doṇhāra gāy*
sucitrā jubatī,　　　　　koriyā ākuti,
*　　nānā citra kore tāy*

"Ratna Mañjarī brought sandalwood pulp and anointed the bodies of the Divine Pair, and the young girl Sucitrā eagerly painted different pictures on Their bodies."

yūthi manohāre,   gāṇthiyā dohāre
porāilo tilottamā
vinoda bandhāne,   sājāiyā du jane,
hariṣa sakala rāmā

"**Tilottamā strung garlands of captivating Yūthi-flowers and hung them around Their necks. All the other girls blissfully decorated the Divine Pair with a delightful style.**"

kadalī panasa,   ati se surasa,
ānalo labaṅga latā
doṇhāre bhojana,   korāe tokhona,
sundarī madana madā

"**Labaṅga-latā brought very juicy bananas and jackfruits and beautiful Madana Madā then fed Them Their meal.**"

vilāsa ālasa,   chuṭalo sakala,
surasa bhojana kori
ācamana kori,   nāgara nāgarī,
tāmbūle vadana pūri

"**They gave up Their loving fatigue by eating juicy foods. After washing Their mouths, Nāgara Kṛṣṇa and Nāgarī Rāi filled Their mouths with betelleaves.**"

sakhīgaṇa saṅge,   nānā rasa raṅge,
nāgara nāgarī rohe
dina avasāna,   kori anumāna,
śekhara sabhāre kohe

"**Thus Nāgara Kṛṣṇa enjoyed different tasty pastimes with Nāgarī Rāi and Her girlfriends. Understanding** that the day has ended, Rāya Śekhara reminds everyone of the same." (85)

🪷

vicchedānurāga
rāgiāī bhāṭiyāri — tāla eka tālā

dina avasāna,   jāniyā parāṇa,
kemon kemon kore
doṇhāra vadana,   nirakhi dujana,
vacana nāhiko sore

"The two lovers stared at Each other's faces, unable to speak a word. Knowing that the day had ended Their hearts were aching so much."

rasika nāgara,   viccheda vibhora,
ghucilo mukhera hāsa
lora jhara jhara,   bol ghara ghara,
khasiyā poroye vāsa

"The smile on the face of Rasika Nāgara (Kṛṣṇa) disappeared at the imminent separation. His voice faltered and tears streamed from His eyes, while His garments dropped from His body."

hiyāy jvalolo,   viccheda analo,
hoi doṅhāra dehā
korite melāni,   ki hoilo nā jāni,
jāgalo dāruṇa lehā

"Their hearts and bodies burned in the fire of separation. I don't know what happened when They took leave of Each other. Intense love arose."

viṣāde viṣaṇṇa,   hoiyā dujan
medinī bhedaye pāy
sakhīgaṇa tathi,   koriyā yugati,
kohoye doṇhāra tāy

"Both became sorrowful and depressed and the earth split under Their feet. The *sakhīs* tried to console Them with their words."

sundarī sundara,   vilamba nā koro,
satvare coloho ghor
avadhi rohile,   ki jāni ki phale,
se āra hoilo ḍor

"O Sundara (Kṛṣṇa) and Sundarī (Rādhe)! Don't delay, but quickly return home! Who knows what will happen when You become late? There will be even more anxiety then!"

śuniyā vacana,   tarāse tokhon,
mandira bāhire āsi
duḥkita hiyāy,   hoilo vidāy
bāṛhilo vedanā rāśi

"Hearing these words They became greatly afraid and came out of Their abode. With aching hearts They took leave of Each other, thus increasing Their great heartache."

catura nāgara,   āilā satvara,
mililā sakhāra saṇge
loiyā maṇḍali,   colilā dulālī,
śekhara colilo raṇge

"Our clever Hero then quickly rejoined His pals while Bhānu Dulālī also went off, taking Her *sakhī-maāḍalī* along. Rāya Śekhara blissfully went with them." (86)

❁

śrī rādhāra gṛhāgamana
rāgiāī pūravī — tāla eka tāla

nijālaye,　　　sakhi saṇhe,
*　　cole sudhāmukhī*
premānale,　　　hiyā jvole,
*　　cholo cholo āṇkhi*

"Sudhāmukhī (nectar-faced Rāi) went home with Her *sakhīs*, Her heart burning in the fire of love and tears trickling from Her eyes."

aṅgera vasana,　　khasaye saghana,
*　　buke dukha bhorā*
mukhe kothā,　　　kohite byathā
*　　hoilā bāuli pārā*

"Her garments slipped off Her body and Her heart was filled with pain. Through Her mouth She spoke of Her pain and She had become like a mad woman."

dhanira bharama,　　dekhiyā karama,
*　　kohiche sakala sakhī*
gopata kothā,　　　bekata korobo,
*　　emata tomāy dekhi*

"When they saw all of Rāi's distorted activities, the *sakhīs* said: 'When You are seen like this Your secrets will be revealed.'"

śītala buke,   thākoho sukhe,
tāp tulicho kene
piyāy loiyā,   hiyāy thuiyā,
khelibe rāti dine

"Blissfully stay here with a cool heart. Why should You be afflicted? Place Your beloved in Your heart and play with Him there day and night."

sakhīra vāṇī,   śuniyā dhani,
āśa bāndhiyā cite
śekhara loiyā,   ghare giyā,
bosilā buṛira bhite

"Hearing the words of Her *sakhīs*, Dhani Rāi cultivated some hope in Her heart. Rāy śekhara then took Her home, where She sat down in fear of Jaṭilā." (87)

❁

gṛha praveśa, sandhyāya snāna
bhūpālī — tāla rūpaka

satī kulavatī,   sakala jubatī,
rādhāre āniyā ghore
parama jatane,   madhura vacane,
sompilo jaṭilā kore

"All the young housewives took Rādhā home and most carefully placed Her back in Jaṭilā's hands, speaking sweet words to her."

hariṣe vadane,   jaṭilā tokhone,
sabāra koriyā mān
ādara bādare,   binoy vebhāre,
deyalo karpūra pān

"Jaṭilā's face beamed with bliss and she greatly praised all the *sakhīs*. Humbly and attentively she present-ed them with camphor-laced betel leaves."

> *dubāhu tuliyā,   devatā ḍākiyā,*
> *   saghane āśīṣa kore*
> *praṇami jaṭilā,   sabhāi colilā*
> *   āpana āpana ghore*

"Lifting both her arms she called upon the demigods and heartily offered blessings. After offering obeisances unto Jaṭilā all the *sakhīs* went to their individ-ual homes."

> *deva roṣa heri,   bhoye bhīta burī,*
> *   manete vicāra kore*
> *deva yāra vaśa,   michā apayaśa,*
> *   nā bujhi deyaluṇ tāre*

"Seeing that the gods were angry, the old hag became afraid and thought to herself: I falsely defamed She who subdues the Lord, but didn't understand it."

> *porera vacane,   hoiyā acetane,*
> *   korinu dāruṇa kāj*
> *dekhinu nayāne,   śuninu śravaṇe,*
> *   māthāy pāṛito bāj*

"I lost my intelligence when I heard others' words (gossip) and I acted cruelly. Now I saw with my own eyes and I heard with my own ears— let a thunderbolt strike my head!"

> *bhālo bole biṭi,   koriyā āṇkhṭi,*
> *   mānāilo nārāyaṇ*

tehi se āmār, rohilo saṁsār,
  putra poribāra dhan

"Biṭi (the old woman) spoke well, respectfully honouring śrī Nārāyaṇa. This girl stayed in my family as its jewel and the jewel for my son."

vadhura marama, charama jāniyā,
  buṛi se kātare bole
o mora dulāli, parāṇa putalī
  sināho śītala jale

'Knowing the heart of her daughter-in-law to be sublime, Jaṭilā anxiously exclaimed: "O my little girl! O Doll of my heart! Bathe in cold water!"

śāśuṛi ādara, dekhiyā sabāra,
  upajilo mahā raṅge
rāi kori cholā, virale bosilā,
  śekhara bosilā saṅge

"Rāi went and sat down in a solitary place, along with Rāya śekhara. Everyone was having great fun in seeing the great respect She received from Her mother-in-law." (88)

pakkānna racanā lāvaāyāmṛta snāna

śāśuḍī sarase, haraṣa hoiyā,
  bhavane bosiyā bālā
surasa pakkānna, korolo racana
  pūralo sonāra thālā

"Rāi sat at home, very happy to see how favorable Her mother-in-law had become. She prepared delicious cooked rice and filled golden trays with it."

ḍhākiyā vasane, rākhiyā gopaṇe,
  sināna korite jāy
dāsīgaṇa saṇge, nānā rasa raṇge,
  sināna korolo tāy

"Covering these preparations with sheets and concealing them, She went off to take a bath, enjoying different tasty pastimes, with the assistance of Her maidservants."

veśera mandire, paśilā satvare,
  korilā mohana veśa
uṭhiyā aṭṭālī, caudike nehāri
  divasa hoilo śeṣa

"She quickly entered Her dressing room and dressed Herself in a captivating way. Then She mounted the roof of the mansion and looked all around. The day was ending."

tulasī ḍākiyā, gopana koriyā,
  deolo lāḍura thālā
aguru candana, āra guyā pān
  sugandhi phulera mālā

"Secretly She called Tulasī and handed her the plate with *laḍḍus*, *aguru*, *pān*, sandalwood pulp and fragrant flower garlands."

śekhara sarasi, śikhāya tulasī,
  dhariyā tāhāra hāta

> *dhaniṣṭhā miliyā,   āsiho coliyā,*
> *bujhiyā saṅketa bāt*

"Tulasī teaches Rāya Śekhara by holding his hand. Go and meet with Dhaniṣṭhā, understanding the verbal hint." (89)

śrī Kṛṣṇa priyāra utkaāṭhā

> *hariṇa nayanī dhanī,   cakita nehārinī,*
> *chala chala unamata bhelā*
> *svajana sohāgana,   tanu mana jīvana,*
> *satinī koriyā bihi delā*

"Fawn-eyed Dhanī Rāi looked around restlessly, gradually becoming completely mad. Fate had turned the love of Her friends, relatives and superiors on the one side and Her body, Her mind and Her life on the other side into Her co-wives (enemies)."

> *kṣaṇe kṣaṇe uṭhato,   kṣaṇe kṣaṇe baiṭhato,*
> *utapata tejalo śvāsā*
> *kṣaṇe kṣaṇe camakai,   kṣaṇe kṣaṇe kampai,*
> *gadagada kohotohi bhāṣā*

"Sometimes She got up, sometimes She sat down and sometimes She breathed deeply. Sometimes She was startled, sometimes She shivered and sometimes She spoke with faltering voice."

> *kula guṇa gaurava,   satī yaśa saurabha,*
> *vāma pāye ṭhelalu tāya*
> *dāruṇa prema theho,   tila nāhi mānato,*
> *palake palake tala pāya*

"With Her left foot She kicked against the fragrant pride of Her dynasty's glories and Her own chastity. Out of great love (for Kṛṣṇa) She didn't care about them at all anymore".

aruṇita locana,   lore bharu ānana,
piyā patha herato rāi
śiśu paśu saṅgata,   kori hari āota,
go kṣura dhūli uchalāi

"Rāi's eyes were red and tears streamed over Her face when She saw Her beloved Hari coming down the road with His cowherd boyfriends and His cows, that threw up dust with their hooves."

kohe kavi śekhara,   dhani puna heraho,
āota nāgara rāja
tuyā mana mānasa,   eto khone pūrabo,
herobi panthaki mājha

Kavi Śekhara says: "Look again, my girl! Your Nāgara rāja (king of heroes) is coming. Your desires will be fulfilled right now when You see Him on the road!" (90)

rāgiāī suhai — tāla eka tālā

dūrete āoto nāgara rāy; jubatī umati unnata cāy
virasa vadana sarasa bhelo; hiyāra āguni tokhoni gelo
hasita vekata vacana miṭh; sajala chuṭalo tarala diṭh
muralī khuralī śunite pāi; atula ānande ākula rāi
dekhibāre sab sakhini jāi; uṭhali aṭṭāli milali rāi
ratana āsane bosilā sabe; śekhara sabāre sevaye tabe

"Nāgara Rāya approached from afar, making the young girls look up to Him, mad with joy. Their wilted faces became juicy once more and the fire of separation that burned in their hearts had disappeared. They spoke sweet words with smiling faces and their restless eyes emitted streams of tears. When She heard the sweet song of Kṛṣṇa's flute, Rāi became agitated with matchless bliss. All Her *sakhīs* then came to see Her on the roof of the mansion. As everyone sat down on jewelled seats, Rāya śekhara engaged in their service." (91)

aparāhna līlā-uttara goṣṭha
rāgiāī māyūra — tāla eka tāla

jāni dina avasān,   colilā catura kān,
praveśilā kadalī kānane
śubala maṅgala saṅge,   jāy nānā rasa raṅge
kadalī loiyā jane jane

"Knowing the day was over, clever Kṛṣṇa went and entered a banana-orchard. There He blissfully picked bananas with Subala and Madhumaṅgala."

mililā sabāra sāthe,   kadalī deolo hāte,
khāy sabe hariṣa hoiyā
poriyā bonera phul,   gāy mākhe rāṅgā dhūl,
dilo gābhī turite hāṅkiyā

"They met all the other boys and handed them all bananas, which they began to eat in great merriment. Dressing themselves in forest flowers and anointing their bodies with colored pigments and dust they quickly proceeded to call the cows."

dhenu sob ghara mukhe,   colilā parama sukhe,
*   ubha karṇa ubha puccha kori*
nāciyā nāciyā jāy,   śiśugaṇa pāche dhāy,
*   dhūlāy gagana gelo bhori*

"The cows all blissfully returned home with raised ears and tails, filling the sky with dust thrown up by their hooves, while the cowherd boys danced behind them."

śiṅgā diyā cāṇda mukhe,   balāi dhavalī hāṅke,
*   mada bhare ḍākena saghan*
athira caraṇa gati,   ghūrṇita nayāna bhāti
*   gada gada nā sphure vacan*

"Holding His horn to His moon-like mouth, Balarāma loudly called the cows, deluded by intoxication. His gait was unsteady and His eyes were rolling, and His words were not clearly audible due to His stuttering voice."

kaṇalī bāchurī kāndhe,   cole matta gaja chānde,
*   ghana ḍāke kānāiyā kānāiyā*
veṇu śāne dhenu hāṅk,   sabhākāra mājhe thāk
*   bone pāche rohibe bhuliyā*

"Keeping a rope for binding the calves on His shoulder He walked like a mad elephant, loudly calling out: "Kānāi! Kānāi!" Calling His cows with His flute He stayed in the middle of the group, lest He would not stay behind in the forest, forgetting to go home."

siṅgā veṇu ek tān,   koriyā deoalo śān
*   śunalo vrajera sab lok*
mātā pitā haraṣita,   kulavadhū pulakita,
*   ghucilo sabhāra dukha śok*

"The boys' horns and flutes played in the same note and all the people of Vraja heard it. Mother Yaśodā and father Nanda were delighted and the *gopīs* had goosepimples of ecstasy all over their bodies. Thus everyone forgot their sorrow and lamentation."

jāvaṭ grāmer kāche, sabe nija dhenu bāche
* vidāy hoilo jane jane*
śekhara satvara kori, kohe śuno sundarī,
* milaho nāgara ei-khone*

"When the cowherd boys reached the village of Jāvaṭ, they sorted out their groups of cows and took leave of one another. Rāy Śekhara then hastened Rāi, saying: "Hear me, O Sundari— now go and meet Your Nāgara!" (92)

sandhyāya śrī rādhā-kṛṣāer premonmāda
śrī rāga — tāla daśa kusi

rādhikā cakorī hāsi, śyāma sane mile āsi
* piye sudhā haraṣita mone*
dūre doṇhā duhuṇ dekhi, pālṭite nāre āṇkhi
* hānilo kusuma śara bāṇe*

"Smiling Rādhikā came to meet Śyāma like a thirsty Cakorī-bird, blissfully drinking the nectar (from His moon like face). Seeing Each other from afar, They could not even blink with Their eyes, as They were hit by Cupid's floral arrows."

avaśa hoilo gā, colite nā cole pā,
* pulake pūralo duhuṇ tanu*

śubala samaya jāni, hāt sāne bodhi dhani
  loiyā colilā tabe kānu

"They became overwhelmed and stunned and could not move one foot anymore. Their bodies were studded with goosepimples. Subala, understanding it was time, took Kṛṣṇa along with him, making a gesture to Rādhā with his hands.

khorike rākhiyā gāi, rāma kṛṣṇa ghore jāi,
  praṇamilo jananī caraṇe
jaśodā cumbana kore, dekhite nā pāy lore,
  āśīṣ koroye dui jane

"Keeping the cows in the meadows, Kṛṣṇa and Balarāma went home and offered Their obeisances unto mother Yaśodā's feet. Yaśodā kissed Them and blessed Them, unable to see anything due to her tear-filled eyes."

rāi jāi bosi ghore, pāṭhāilo tulasīre
  marama kohiyā tāra kāṇe
sakhīgaṇa loiyā rādhā, pūraye monera sādhā,
  se sab lakhite nāre āne

"Rāi went back home and sat down there. She then sent for Tulasī and spoke confidential matters into her ear. The *sakhīs* took Rādhā along and satisfied Her desires, unnoticed by anyone else."

tulasī ulasi hoiyā, jāy upahāra loiyā,
  turite paśilo rāja-ghare
gopate loiyā thālā, dhaniṣṭhāre diyā bālā,
  kohilo rāiyera samācāre

"Tulasī quickly and blissfully went to the abode of Nanda Mahārāja, taking different ingredients with her. This young girl handed the tray with dishes to Dhaniṣṭhā and secretly told her the latest news about Rāi."

jāniyā rādhār marma,   śekhare koroye karma,
vichānā vichāy koto bhāti
sakhīgaṇa loiyā sāthe,   bosi rasavati tāte,
tulasīr koriyā avadhi

"Knowing Rādhā's feelings, Rāya Śekhara performed his duty by making Her bed. Taking Her *sakhīs* along, Rasavatī Rāi sat down there, waiting for Tulasī." (93)

❀

sāyaṁ kāla—ārāti
gaurī — tāla eka tālā

jaśomati ārati koroto vidhāne;
gurukula maṇgala korotohi gāne
sukha bhare dvijagaṇe koru bahu dāne;
dāsagaṇe ṭoikhone colu nija kāme
vedi'pora ko dhoru śītala nīre;
koi loi āolo pātala cīre
keho lei dui bhāi vedite bosāi;
ratana bhūṣaṇa puna jatane khosāi
rāma-kānu dohe puna pahiralo cīre;
go-dhūli dhoyalo śītala nīre

"As mother Yaśodā performed Kṛṣṇa's *sandhyā ārati*, Kṛṣṇa's elderly relatives sang auspicious songs. Kṛṣṇa then blissfully gave profuse charity to the *brāhmaāas* and His servants went to render their own serv-

ices. Some of them bathed the two brothers (Kṛṣṇa-Balarāma) with cold water, others brought thin towels (to dry Them off). Some brought Them to the bathing platform and seated Them there while others carefully peeled Their garments and ornaments off Their bodies. Some brought in Their fresh clothes and some washed the cowdust off Their bodies with cold water."

> keho dei duhuṅ aṅge ubaṭana gandhe;
> sughaḍa sevaka mardaye koto raṅge
> sugandhi salile puna korolo sināne;
> duhuṅ aṅga mochaye sevaka sujāne
> nīla pīta vasana poroli duhuṅ raṅge;
> sugandhi candana keho lepoi aṅge
> koho kavi śekhara kori anumāne;
> baiṭhalo duhuṅ taba koriyā sināne

"Some applied scented *udvartanas* (powders to remove unguents) to Their bodies, and other expert servants blissfully massaged Them. Some bathed Them again with fragrant water and other saintly servants wiped off Their bodies. Some servants dressed Them in blue and yellow garments and some anointed Their bodies with fragrant sandalwood pulp. Rāya śekhara thinks to himself: "When They sit down I will bathe Them." (94)

> *pradoṣa līlā*
> *rāgiāī imana — tāla eka tālā*

> samay jāniyā,   turite hoiyā,
>   āsiyā dhaniṣṭhā nārī
> jaśodā mandire,   piṇḍāra upore,
>   sukhada āsana kori

"Knowing the time to be proper, Dhaniṣṭhā quickly came and made a blissful seat on a platform in Yaśodā's abode."

sugandhi salila, koriyā śītala,
*   pūriyā ānalo jhāri*
rāiko pakkānna, āniyā tokhona,
*   rākhalo pṛthako kori*

"She then brought a jug of cold, scented water along with Rāi's cooked food and kept them in separate places."

e sūpa mudga, moricā sukhada,
*   ye kichu āchilo ghare*
yaśodā vacane, ānilā tokhone,
*   kānura bhojana tore*

"On Yaśodā's order she brought whatever delicacies there were in the house for Kṛṣṇa's supper— soup of *dāl*, delightful black pepper, etc."

sināna koriyā, bolāi hāsiyā,
*   colilā āpane ghare*
kānura vacana, nā māne tokhona,
*   vāruṇī pānera tare*

"Balarāma laughed as He bathed and went to His own room. He did not bother about Kṛṣṇa's words then, since He went to drink His Vāruṇī wine."

hāsiyā tokhone, sukhada āsane,
*   bosilā jādava rāy*
māyera pirīte, lāgilā bhuñjite,
*   tulasī koroye bāy*

"Then Yādava Rāya (Kṛṣṇa) carefully sat down on His delightful chair and was fed by His loving mother, while Tulasī fanned Him."

> *jananī binoye,　　śunoho tanoye,*
> 　*ār nā bolibo ki*
> *tomār kāroṇa,　　e sab pakkānna,*
> 　*pāṭhāy rājhāra jhi*

"Mother Yaśodā humbly said: "Hear me, O son—what more can I say? For Your sake Princess Rādhā has sent all these cooked and fried dishes.""

> *aruci tejiyā,　　bhojana koriyā,*
> 　*ghucāho sabāra dukh*
> *tomāra bhojana,　　śuniyā tokhona,*
> 　*rādhikā pāobo sukh*

"Give up your weak appetite and eat, effacing everyone's misery. When Rādhikā hears that You're eating, She will be very happy."

> *māyera vacane,　　nandera nandana,*
> 　*buñjalo parama sukhe*
> *uṭhi ācamane,　　korolo jatane,*
> 　*tāmbūla deolo mukhe*

"Hearing His mother's words, Nanda-nandana began to eat in topmost bliss. Then He got up, carefully washed His mouth and placed a betelleaf in it."

> *kānura vadana,　　nirakhe saghana,*
> 　*dhaniṣṭhā caturī bālā*
> *iṅgita bujhiyā,　　catura nāgara,*
> 　*deolo campaka mālā*

"The clever girl Dhaniṣṭhā stared at Kṛṣṇa's face. Understanding her hint, the clever Nāgara gave her a Campaka-garland."

saṅket koriyā, dhaniṣṭhā āniyā,
deolo tulasī kore
avaśeṣa loiyā, thālite bhoriyā,
deolo rāiera tore

"Dhaniṣṭhā then winked at Tulasī and handed her the garland. Tulasī then took the remnants from Kṛṣṇa's meal on a tray to give them to Rāi."

se sob loiyā, tulasī coliyā,
turite āolo ghore
thālā mālā tathi, tulasī juvatī,
sompilo rādhāra kore

"Taking all this along, Tulasī quickly went (to Rādhā's) home. Young Tulasī then delivered the tray and the garland in Rādhā's hands."

saṅketa kāhinī, bujhilā taruṇī,
campaka mālāṭi dekhi
tāmbūla biṭikā, deolo rādhikā,
tuṣilo sakala sakhī

"When young Rādhā saw the Campak-garland She understood Kṛṣṇa's indication on the night's rendez vous. Rādhikā then pleased all Her *sakhīs* by distributing betel-leaves."

nānā rasa gāna, kori sakhīgaṇa,
colilā āpana ghore

samoy jāniyā,   thālā mālā loiyā,
śekhara gopana kore

"The sakhīs sang different rasika songs and then returned to their individual abodes. Knowing the time was proper, Rāya Śekhara then took the tray and the garland and concealed them." (95)

❁

go dohana
rāga- kāmoda

jala pāna kori kān,   mukhe diyā guyā pān
khaḍike colilā go dohane
gābhi-gaṇa stana bhore,   ghana hamvāraba kore
kānu patha nirakhe saghane

"After enjoying a snack, Kṛṣṇa placed a betelleaf in His mouth and went out into the meadows to milk His cows. The cows bellowed loudly because their udders were full and Kṛṣṇa's eyes scanned the pathways."

āilā gokula cānd,   kore dhari ḍori chānd,
āra gopa āsi tāra saṅge
chāṛi dilā vatsa sab,   goṭhe uṭhe hāmvārab
śunite bāṛhilo bahu raṅge

"Kṛṣṇa, the moon of Gokula, came with a rope for tying up the calves, and the other cowherd boys accompanied Him. When they released the calves the whole meadow was filled with bellowing and mooing, hearing which everyone felt increasing joy."

dekhiyā kānura mukha,   dhenura hoilo sukha,
vatsa piye haraṣita mane

piśaṇgī māṇikya stanī,   dohe kānu guṇamaṇi
āra gābhi dohe gopa gaṇe

"Seeing Kṛṣṇa's face the cows became very happy and their calves drank in great joy. Kṛṣṇa, the jewel of attributes, milked Piśaṇgī and Māāikya-stanī while the other cowherd boys milked the other cows."

dohana koriyā sārā,   saṇge loiyā dugdha bhārā
rākhilā māyera kāche jāi
aṭṭālīte hoiyā khāṛā,   śekhara bujhilā sārā
dohana hoilo saba gāi

"After milking all the cows they carried the load of milk home together, kept it with mother Yaśodā and left. Standing on the roof of the mansion Rāya Śekhara understood that all the cows have been milked." (96)

❀

śrī rāma-kṛṣāera sabhāya gamana
dhānaśī — tāla lophā

śiropari lāl jari bāndhe juvarāj;
śruti-mūle kuṇḍala manohara sāj
nāsā pāśe moti nolake jhalakāy;
sūkṣma sutalī puna deolo gāy
maṇimoy hāra śobhe kaṇṭhaka mājh;
ura para ratanaka padaka virāj
kaṭihuṇ kāṭāri paṭukā koru bandh;
bhālohi śobhita candana cand
haladhara dhari koro colu darbār;
āge pāche jāy kāche dāsa parivār
duhuṇ meli baiṭhali vraja-rāja pāś;
sabhājana rañjana sarasa sambhāṣ

koho kobi śekhara samoya vicār;
sabhā mājhe boiṭholo rāja kumār

"The prince bound a red and golden string around His head and His earlobes were decorated with captivating earrings. A pearl was hung under His nose with a string and more thin strings were hung on His body. A jewelled necklace beautified His neck and a jewelled locket adorned His chest. (For the social occasion) .He wore a dagger in a sash around His waist and His forehead was beautified by spots of sandalwood pulp. Holding Haladhara (Balarāma)'s hand He entered the assembly, with servants walking before and behind Him. Both Kṛṣṇa and Balarāma met Vrajarāja Nanda and sat by His sides, pleasing the assembled elders with sweet words. Kavi śekhara, considering the time, says: "Thus Prince Kṛṣṇa sat down in the assembly." (97)

gīta vādyādi śravaāa
rāgiāī maṅgala — tāla gaḍakhemaṭā

guṇigaṇa kore gān,   loiyā vividha tān,
vādya padya ati manohar
nācaye nartaka tathi,   jiniyā khañjana gati,
dekhi sabe hariṣa antar

"The panegyrists sang in different tunes, performing prose songs in a very enchanting way with their musical instruments. The dancers danced more friskily than wagtail-birds, seeing which everyone became happy at heart."

gāna vādya nṛtya rase,   sabāi ānande bhāse
punaḥ puna kore āsvādane

diyā rājā bahu dhana,   tuṣilen guṇigaṇa,
*   tār pāche dilo kavigaṇe*

"Everyone drowned in transcendental bliss while repeatedly relishing the mellows of singing, dancing and playing musical instruments. Mahārāja Nanda gave a lot of charity to satisfy the panegyrists and after that he gave wealth to the poets."

peṭa moṭā ṭheṭā bhāṭa,   gāna vādya rākhi nāṭa
*   rāybāra pore tvarātvari*
āsiyā bhānṛera ṭhāṭ,   juri hāta vinoda nāṭ,
*   duṇhe mili kore huṛāhuṛi*

"An impudent pot-bellied minstrel sang and played musical instruments in a drama and quickly recited praises. With folded hands a clown came and performed a funny show. The two then met and jostled."

hāsi hāsi rāma kānu,   kautuka dekhaye punu,
*   tāra mājhe pheli dilo dhan*
bhānṛe bhāṭe kāṛākāṛi,   mārāmāri pāṛāpāṛi,
*   kautuka dekhaye sabhā-jan*

"Balarāma and Kṛṣṇa laughed and viewed the fun again. In between They threw coins. The public then witnessed in amusement how the clowns snatched things away from each other, beat each other and plucked at each other."

tabe to dekhiyā rāti,   raktaka āsiyā tathi,
*   kohilo rājāra kāne kāne*
mātā pāṭhāilo more,   nite rāma dāmodare
*   turite koroho samādhāne*

"Then, seeing that night had fallen, Raktaka came there and whispered into Nanda Mahārāja's ears— "Mother sent me to take Balarāma and Dāmodara along. Quickly stop the show."

nanda eto bol śuni,   bhānre bhāṭe ḍāki āni,
dhana diyā ghucāilo dukha
prajāgaṇe āśvāsiyā,   rāma dāmodara loiyā,
ghare gelo kori mahāsukha

"Hearing these words, Nanda Mahārāja called the clowns to him and removed their sorrow by giving them a lot of money. Then, after consoling his subjects, he took Balarāma and Dāmodara along and proceeded home in great bliss."

dekhi śuni nṛtya gīta,   ānande magana cita,
sabhājana nija ghare jāy
āsi rāma dāmodara,   bosilā piṇrāra por,
samaye śekhara guṇa gāy

"All the assembled spectators then blissfully went home, having heard and seen this singing and dancing. Meanwhile Balarāma and Dāmodara took Their seats (in Their private quarters) and Rāya śekhara sings Their glories according to the time." (98)

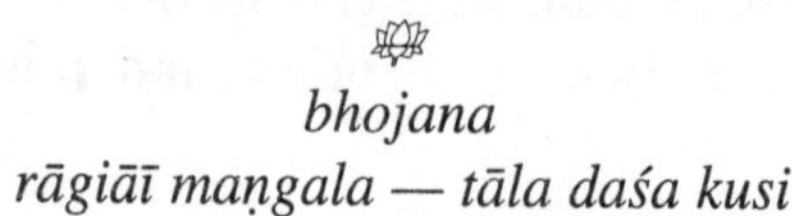

bhojana
rāgiāī maṅgala — tāla daśa kusi

sevaye sevaka-gaṇa,   ānande ākula mana,
leho sukhe pāsare āpanā
rāma dāmodara vine,   āra kichu nāhi jāne,
sevā sukhe satata maganā

"In the course of their devotional service the servants of Kṛṣṇa forgot themselves in transcendental loving bliss. They don't know anything else but Balarāma and Dāmodara and they are always immersed in the bliss of devotional service."

āste vyaste alaṅkāra,   ghucāilo doṅhākāra,
*   bhojanera vasana porāiyā*
caraṇa pākhāli nīre,   mochilo pātala cīre,
*   bhojana bhavana jāy loiyā*

"They busily removed the ornaments from the Two Brothers and dressed Them in eating clothes. They then washed Their feet with water, dried them off with thin towels and took Them to the dining room."

raktaka pavitra kori,   pāte piṇṛā sāri sāri
*   pūri jhāri suśītala nīre*
rāma dāmodara āsi,   piṇṛāra upore bosi,
*   bāp ke bolāya bāre bāre*

"With clean hands Raktaka placed rows of low chairs and filled glasses with cold water. Balarāma and Dāmodara then came, sat upon the chairs and repeatedly called Their father."

nanda upānanda ādi   bhojane bosilā āsi,
*   rāma kānu loiyā dui pāśe*
dudha bhāt pūribo belā,   jaśodā āniyā dilā
*   āra koto sumadhura rase*

"Nanda, his elder brother Upānanda and others then sat down to eat, taking Balarāma and Kṛṣṇa on their flanks. Mother Yaśodā then brought trays with milk and rice and so many very sweet juices."

khīr pūri bhori thālā,   sabāre āniyā dilā
bhojana koroye mahā-sukhe
doṇhāra bhojana dekhi,   mātāra śītala āṅkhi
ghucilo manera sab dukhe

"She filled up everyone's plates with *kṣīra* (sweet rice) and *puris*, and everyone began to eat in great bliss. Seeing them eating soothed mother's eyes and removed all her mental anguish."

mā bāper prema rase,   bhuñjilo sakala sukhe,
ghana ghana uṭhibāre cāy
alase avaśa tanu,   hoilen rāma kānu
dekhiyā duḥkita bhelo māy

"Balarāma and Kṛṣṇa blissfully relished the mellows of Their mother and father's love and then got up. Mother Yaśodā was very sad to see Balarāma and Kṛṣṇa overwhelmed by fatigue."

āsiyā sevaka gaṇa,   korāilo ācamana
śayana bhavane loiyā jāy
haladhara niṇda bhore,   colilā āpana ghare
kānāire śayane pāṭhāy

"Then Kṛṣṇa's servants came, helped Him flush His mouth and took Him to His bedroom. Balarāma fell over of sleep and went to His own room after sending Kānāi (Kṛṣṇa) to His bedroom."

nandera nandana kān,   mukhe diyā guyā pān,
bosilā sukhada śejopari
ālase ḍhāliye gā,   sevake sevaye pā,
nidrāy nayān bhelo bhori

"Kṛṣṇa, the son of Mahārāja Nanda, placed a *pān* in His mouth and sat down upon His delightful bed. He reclined His tired body on it while His servants served His feet. Thus His eyes became filled with sleep."

niṇde bhelo acetana,   dekhiyā sevaka gaṇa,
*   āpana āpana ghare jāy*
śekhara samay jāni,   nijālaye kohe dhani,
*   bhojanera koroho upāy*

"Seeing that Kṛṣṇa fell asleep and lost consciousness, His servants went to their individual rooms. Knowing the time, Rāy śekhara went to his/her own abode and told Dhanī Rāi: 'Now go and eat.' (99)

Kṛṣṇa-priyādiger bhojana
rāginī dhānaśī — tāla eka tālā

jaṭilā kohoye badhura ṭhāi; turite bhojana koroho māi
āyāna bhojana koriyā gelo; durmedha kuṭilā śayana koilo
āndhalo nayāna nā suje more; bosite nā pāri niṇdera bhore
āpani bāchani koroho sāti; dekhite dekhite bāṛhilo rāti

"Jaṭilā told her daughter-in-law: 'O mother! Quickly come and eat. Your husband has already gone to eat and the foolish Kuṭilā has gone to bed. These blind eyes of mine can hardly see anymore_and I can hardly sit up anymore of sleep. Take Your girlfriends with You—see how the night advances."

tileka soyātha nāhiko tora; nayāna putalī tumi se mora
e ghara karaṇa tohāri hāta; śapatha koroṇ mui jhiyāri māth
devara durmedha koribe mo; āmār āśīṣe hoibe po
kuṭilā pāpinī kondala kore; kāli se jāibe porer ghore

"You don't have the slightest advantage, (still) You are the puppet of my eyes. This house is maintained by Your hand, I swear upon Your head, my daughter! My dull-brained brother-in-law says: 'By my blessings You will get a son'. The sinful Kuṭilā is making quarrels— she will go to another's house tomorrow."

se tāpe tāpita nahibe tore; sakala kubol khomibā more
tomāra bāpera bharasā kori; e tin bhuvane kāre nā ḍori
tomāra mātāra ki kobo kothā; āmāre jānaye āpana dhātā
kuśale thākuk tāhāra put; devatā dānava nā lāgu bhūt
jaṭilā eteko jatana kore; kohoye śekhara devera ḍore

"This anguish will not torment You anymore, forgive me for all the gossip and insults. I trust Your father; I don't fear anyone in the three worlds. What can I say about Your mother? She should know me to be Your protector. May her son be well and not be touched by the demigods, demons or ghosts." Rāya śekhara says: "Jaṭilā does all this effort out of fear of the gods." (100)

rāginī dhānaśī — tāla eka tāla

hede āra kothā śunoho jhi!
kohite kohite bhuliyāchi

"O hear me, my daughter-in-law! While speaking I have forgotten!"

āguni lāguka āmār mone; rahite nāriye kohiye mene
tanaya āyān geyāne dorho; tomāra mātāke ḍorāy boro
devatā samāna mānaye tāy; kohite siñciyā poṛoye gāy
taper phalete devatā vaś; tehi se bhuvane ghoṣaye jaś

"Let my mind catch fire. I think I will not stay around much longer. My knowledge is fixed in my son āyān, I greatly fear (respect) Your mother. I consider her to be equal to a demigod. As I say this, my body is sprinkled (by tears). As a result of penances she has subdued the gods, who are now announcing her fame in the world."

jarati kohiyā pirīti bāt; hāsiyā dharilā badhūra hāt
uṭhilā rādhikā colilā saṅge; randhana bhavane pośilā raṅge

"Thus Jaṭilā spoke loving words to Rādhikā, smiling at Her and holding Her hand. Rādhikā got up and went along with Her, blissfully entering the kitchen."

jaṭilā kohoye boisaho jhi; āmi sab tore āniyā di
khīr puri bhāt dudhera belā; jatane jaṭilā badhūre dilā

"Jaṭilā said: "O daughter, sit down! I will bring You everything!" Thus Jaṭilā carefully served her daughter-in-law sweet rice, *puris*, rice and milk."

minati koriyā kohoye rāi; āpani śayana koroho māi
āpanāra ghare jāiye loiyā; koribo bhojana soyātha pāiyā
śuniyā jaṭilā pāilo sukha; hāsiyā cumbilā vadhūra mukha
bhāloi kohilā o mora mā; āmār kemona koriche gā

"Humbly Rāi said: "O mother, now go to bed. I will take My meal to My own room and thus find peace. When Jaṭilā heard this, she became very happy. She smiled and kissed her daughter-in-law's face, saying: "You spoke very well, O my mother (Rādhā). How could I go (without Your request to do so)?"

jaṭilā jāiyā śayana kore; rādhikā āilā āpana ghare;
āniyā vasane gopana kori; mandirera kone rākhilā dhari
śekhara dhoyāy sakhaṛā hāt; kohite avaśa āulāya gāt

"Jaṭilā went to take rest and Rādhikā went to to Her own room. Secretly She brought Her clothes and kept them in a corner of the house. śekhara washed the food remnants (*sakhaḍa*) from Her hand, his body becoming stunned by ecstatic love." (101)

❀

rāgiāī suhai — tāla eka tālā

ratana mañjarī jatana kori; ratana āsana pātala sāri
sugandhi salile pūriyā jhāri; āsana nikaṭe rākhilo dhari
lavaṅga mañjarī lāṛura thālā; āniyā dhorilo dudhera belā
dadhi kadalaka ācāra joto; prithaka koriyā rākhilo koto

"Ratana Mañjarī carefully spread a *sāri* (sheet) over a jewelled throne, filled a jug with fragrant water and kept it next to the throne. Labaṅga Mañjarī brought a tray with *laḍḍus*, placed a pitcher with milk next to it, and kept so many kinds of yoghurt, bananas and pickles in separate places."

āsiyā āsane bosilā rādhā; dekhite pūraye manera sādhā
kānu avaśeṣa paraśa pāi; amiyā sāgare sāṇtāre rāi
pulaka pūralo rāiko tanu; piyā rasa madhu pāyalo janu
adhara athira bhāvera bhore; bharame bhūlilo bhuñjite nāre

"Rādhā came and sat down on the throne. Seeing the arrangements, Her desires were fulfilled. Rāi swam in an ocean of nectar simply by touching Kṛṣṇa's remnants. Rāi's body was studded with goosepimples as She drank the honey of Her beloved's remnants. Her lips trembled of deep ecstasy and She became so overwhelmed that She forgot to continue Her meal."

tarala nayāne bhorolo lora;
jugala aṅgule bhuñjaye thor
nā kore bhojana nā cole koro;
mañjarī lavaṅge upaje ḍoro
madana mañjarī madane matā;
madhura madhura kohoye kothā
emone kemone jāibe din;
ithe ki bujhiye bhālera cin

"Tears trickled from Her restless eyes and with two fingers She ate a little more. Then She could not eat, nor could She move Her hands. This made Labaṅga Mañjarī apprehensive. Madana Mañjarī was intoxicated by amorous desires (in *bhāva-tādātmya* with śrī Svāminījī) and spoke ever-so-sweet words: "How will You pass the day like this? Can I thus understand the signs on Your forehead (Your fate)?"

satvare sakala bhuñjaho rāi; samaye saṅkete jāite cāi
raṅgavatī guṇa mañjarī sāthe; kohoto lalitā āsiche pathe

"Rāi! Quickly eat up everything if You still wish to arrive at the meeting-place in time! Just see! Lalitā is coming here already, in the company of Raṅgavatī and Guāa Mañjarī!"

viśākhā viṣāde āsiche dhāiye; rasavatīgaṇera śabada pāiye
ihāte kemon koribo kāj; sundarī roholo gharera mājh

"Viśākhā comes running over here in a morose mood, hearing the *rasavatī sakhīs*. How can I work like this, as long as Sundarī remains at home?"

āmrā sabhāi rabhasa sāthi; chuṭalo avadhi uṭhalo rāti
śuniyā kāminī kapaṭa kalā; tarāse bhuñjalo sakali bālā

"We are all playful companions. It is time. Night has come." Hearing this, Kāminī Rādhā showed false dexterity and quickly ate everything."

āñcāi āñcale muchalo mukha; tāmbūla khāiyā pāyalo sukha
sukhada pālaṅke śutalo rāi; śekhara śeṣe bhuñjalo jāi

"With the edge of Her *sārī* She wiped Her mouth and blissfully ate a *pān*. Then Rāi reclined on a blissful bedstead. Rāya śekhara relishes all this in the end (or: relishes Her remnants)." (102)

❀

madhya-rātri
rāgiāī kalyāāī — tāla eka tālā

yamunā puline,   campaka kānane,
vilāsa mandira sāje
vṛndā vidhu-mukhī,   vinoda vichānā,
korolo tāhāra mājhe

"On the bank of Yamunā, in a forest of Campaka-flowers, is a play-cottage which is decorated with a pleasure-bed by moon-faced Vṛndā."

praphulla kamala,   dala sukomala,
tulira tulanā kori
pālaṅka upori,   pātalo sundarī,
caudige phulera jhuri

"This beautiful goddess picked tender petals from blossoming lotus flowers and hung them suspended all over and around the bedstead."

vicitra vasane,   jhāpilo tokhone,
  bāndhalo pāṭera jāde
pālaṅka du pāśe,   phulera bāliśe,
  deyoli manera sādhe

"She covered the bed with wonderful sheets and bound silken tassles to them. On both sides of the bed she lay flower pillows according to her wish."

mandira bhitore   sugandhi phulera,
  cāṇdoyā bāndhilo tathi
racanā koriyā,   haraṣita hoiyā,
  jvālilo kanaka bāti

"Inside the Mandira she bound a canopy made of fragrant flowers. Then she blissfully lit golden lamps."

karpūra tāmbūla,   jala suśītala,
  rākhalo bhājana bhori
aguru candana,   doṇhāra kāraṇa,
  pūriyā rākhalo khuri

"She kept camphor-laced betelleaves, pitchers filled with cool water and clay cups with *aguru* and sandalwood pulp there also, for Their service."

kānana śobhana,   nā jāy kohono,
  madana koṭāla tāy
phula śara kore,   phiraye sahare,
  kokila pañcama gāy

"The beauty of the forest is indescribable. This room of Cupid was filled with camphor-laced betelleaves and cold water. Cupid wandered around town, wielding his flower arrows, and the cuckoos sang in the fifth note."

sugandhi śītala,   bohoye anila,
parāge pūralo bāṭa
kori madhu pāna,   ali kore gāna,
mayūrī koroye nāṭa

"Fragrant cold breezes blew and the pathways were filled with pollen, the bees sang while they drank honey from the flowers and the peacocks danced."

vṛndā vichānā,   koriyā racanā,
jāgiyā rohilo tāy
śekhara tokhona,   koriyā bhojana,
rāiko nikaṭe jāy

"Vṛndā made a bed and remained awake there. Rāya Śekhara then takes his meal and goes to see Rāi." (103)

rāgiāī bhūpālī — tāla lophā

lalitā viśākhā ādi joto sakhīgaṇa;
tvarī kori kāj sāri pore abharaṇa
sabe sukhī niśi dekhi ghora andhiyār;
leha rase sabe bhāse nā kore vicār
gurujana durujana niṇde acetan;
pāṛāy bujhiye sāṛā nāhi kon jan
caturī ābhirī nāri sabei seyān;
somoy bujhiyā tab korolo payān
rādhār mandire sabe āilā satvare;
śekhara ādar kori bosāy sabāre

"Lalitā, Viśākhā and other *sakhīs* quickly put on their *sārīs* and ornaments. Everyone was blissfully sleeping and the darkness was dense. Everyone was floating in the

mellows of love, forgetting all other considerations. The wicked elders were lying in an unconscious state of sleep and once lulled to sleep no one responded. All the clever cowherd girls thus put up a show; understanding the time was proper they all fled their houses. They all quickly arrived at Rādhā's abode and Rāya śekhara respectfully offered them all seats." (104)

❀

veśābhisāra
rāgiṇī dhānaśī — tāla eka tālā

sakhīgaṇa āgamana,   dekhiyā hariṣa mana,
dhani uṭhi bosi śeja mājhe
nayāna kacāli kore,   mukhāni pākhāle nīre
rajanī samāna kori sāje

"When the *sakhīs* arrived, Dhani Rāi became very glad and got up to sit on Her bed. Rubbing Her eyes and washing Her face with water, She began to dress just like the night[3]."

guṇavatī saba hu je jānaye uddeśa;
madana mohana mana,   mohana kāraṇa,
koru tahi nirupama veśa

"Guāavatī knew exactly what Her purpose was, so she began to dress Her in a matchless manner, just to enchant the mind of the enchanter of Cupid."

kuñcita keśera veṇī,   kālo jāde sājanī,
mṛgamada lepoli aṅge
nīla vasana dhani,   maṇḍita bhelo tani,
nīla bhūṣaṇa pari raṅge

"She decorated Her braid, that consists of curly locks, with a black tassle and anointed Her body with musk. Then She dressed Dhani Rāi with a blue *sārī* and blissfully decorated Her with blue ornaments."

nīla kamala hāte, coṛoli manorathe,
sārathi sāhasa rāje
manamatha bājī, sāji tāhe joṛalo,
toṛalo kula bhaya lāje

"She went according to Her desires, holding a blue lotus flower in Her hand, with great courage. Her dressing was like a magic trick played by Cupid to link Her (to Kṛṣṇa) and tore apart Her virtue and shame."

jubatī ghaṭā loi, baiṭhali rasavatī,
khane khone cita ucāṭe
tab kavi śekhara, hoyalo bāhira,
heraite nāgara bāṭe

"The mind of Rāsavatī Rāi was agitated at every moment. This *rasika* young girl slowed down and sat down. Then Kavi śekhara went out and saw the *nāyaka* (amorous hero Kṛṣṇa) down the road." (105)

rajanī sandhāna
tirotā

sahacari anucari kori anumān;
dehali lāgi bujhe rajanī sandhān
jāgalo nāhi dekhalo eka loka;
sukha saye śutalo nāhi dukha śoka
bāṭaka kaṇṭaka saba bhelo dūr;

sabe ek jāgaye manamatha śūr
nagara nīraba nirajana bāṭ;
durajana nayanahi lāgalo kapāṭ
śekhara kohotohi pantha vicār;
abhisara sundari bhoya nāhi ār

"Looking at the terrace, Her girlfriends and maid-servants understood that night had fallen. No one was seen to be awake anymore; everyone had reclined without any trouble or distress. The thorns on the road had gone far away, only the almighty Cupid remained awake. Nāgara Kṛṣṇa thus silently proceeded over the deserted road while the eyes of the wicked remained shut. As Rāya Śekhara inspects the road he says: "O Sundari! Don't be scared of this love journey anymore!" (106)

❁

Kṛṣṇa priyā gaāera abhisāra
rāgiāī bhūpālī — tala eka tālā

kājara rucihara rajanī viśālā;
tachu por abhisārakoru vraja-bālā
ghara saye nikasaye joichana cor;
niśabada padagati cololi hu thor
unamati cita ati ārati vithāra;
guruyā nitamba nava yauvana bhāra
kamalinī mājhā khini uca kuca jor;
dhādhase colu-koto bhāve vibhor

"The night spread out vastly, stealing the luster of collyrium; in such a night the Vraja-girls went out to rendez-vous with Kṛṣṇa. They left their houses like thieves, their feet moving slowly and silently, and their minds reeling with passionate yearning. Their buttocks were heavy and they also carried a heavy weight of youthful beauty. The waists of these lotus-like girls were slender and their raised breasts were heavy. Greatly agitated they went on, immersed in so many ecstatic feelings."

raṅgiṇī saṅgiṇī nava nava joṛā;
nava anurāgiṇī nava rase bhorā
aṅgaka abharaṇa bāsaye bhār;
nūpura kiṅkiṇī tejalo hār
nīla kamala upekhilo rāmā;
manthara gati coli dhari sakhi śyāmā
jatana hi niḥsaru nagara durantā;
śekhara abharaṇa bhelo vahantā

"The playful girlfriends were all filled with new strength and fresh passion of *rasa*. They carried a heavy weight of ornaments, so they gave up their waistbells, anklebells and necklaces. This woman gave up her blue lotus and Śyāmā-*sakhī* moved on slowly, carrying it. Carefully they left their terrible town while Rāya Śekhara carries their ornaments." (107)

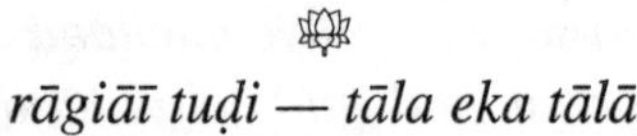

rāgiāī tuḍi — tāla eka tālā

colite nā pāre jauvana bhāre; dhāḍhase dharali sakhīra kore
navīnā kāminī kanaka latā; e tin bhuvane tulanā kothā
satvare saraṇi dharali rāi; nibhṛta nikuñje paśili jāi
kanaka cāmpāra kuñjera mājh; vṛndā korolo vividha sāj

"They could not move swiftly due to the heavy burden of their youthful beauty (heavy buttocks and breasts) holding the hands of their *sakhīs* in agitation. In these three worlds these young girls can only be compared to golden vines. Rāi quickly found the road and entered a solitary grove, which Vṛndā had decorated with different golden Campaka-vines."

vinoda bichānā vinoda bon; dekhite śītala hoilo mon
rādhikā ramaṇī phulera mūle; viśākhā gāṇthiyā deyoli cule
khalita vasana porilā bālā; lalitā deyolo gāṇthiyā mālā

"Her mind was soothed when She saw a pleasure bed in this pleasure forest. Viśākhā strung a garland of flowers and placed it in Rādhikā Ramaāī's hair. One girl straightened out Her scattered clothes and Lalitā gave Her a strung garland."

gāoto kokila madhura gīta; tarala korolo dhanira cita
unmāda madane mātalo mon; caudige beṛholo sakhīra gaṇ
parāṇ piyāre nā dekhi bone; ānalo ujhāli uṭhiche mone
kohoye śekhara śunoho rāi; nāgara vāratā bujhite jāi

"The cuckoos sang sweet songs, making Dhani Rāi's mind restless. Her mind went mad of lust and *sakhīs* surrounded Her on all sides. Not seeing Her heart's beloved in the forest, a fire began to burn in Her heart. Rāya śekhara then said: "Hear me, O Rāi! I am going to find out what's happening with Your *nāgara*!" (108)

kṛṣāābhisāra
śrī rāga — tāla eka tālā

jānalo ghara para niṇde bhelo bhor;
śeja teji uṭhi nanda kiśor
saghane gagane heri nakhatara pāṇti;
avadhi nā jānalo nā uṭhalo rāti
jaladhara ruci hara śyāmara kāṇti;

jubatī mohana veśa dharu koto bhāti
dhani anurāginī jāni sujān;
ghora āndhiyāre taba korolo payān
para nārī pirītika aichana rīt;
colilo nibhṛta pathe nā mānaye bhīt
kusumita kānana kālindī tīra;
tāhā coli āolo gokula bīr
śekhara pantha por milalo jāi;
ānali nāgara bheṭali rāi

"Knowing that everyone else in the house was sleeping, Nanda Kiśora (Kṛṣṇa) got up from bed. He stared at the clusters of stars in the clouded sky, not knowing whether the night had come or not. His bluish luster stole the luster of the monsoon clouds and He dressed Himself in garments that would steal the hearts of the young girls. Knowing that Dhanī Rāi was passionately waiting for Him, He fled into the dark night. Such are the ways of loving other men's wives—thus He went over secret paths without being afraid. Kṛṣṇa, the hero of Gokula, arrived in a flower garden on the bank of Yamunā, where He met with Rāya Śekhara, who escorted Him to Rāi's *kuñja*." (109)

❀

milana
rāgiāī kedāra — tāla lophā

aparūpa rādhā-mādhava meli;
duhuṇ doṇhā daraśane,   ākula antara
amiyā sāyare ḍubi geli

How wonderful is the meeting of Rādhā and Mādhava! When They saw Each other Their anxious hearts merged in an ocean of nectar."

duhu diṭhi duhu mukhe,   avadhi nāhiko sukhe
*   pulake pūralo duhu tanu*
caudike sakhīra ṭhāt,   joichana cāṇder hāt
*   tāra mājhe śobhe rādhā kānu*

"There was no end to Their joy when They beheld Each other's faces, and Their bodies became studded with goosepimples. They were surrounded on all sides by *sakhīs*, that resembled a marketplace of moons. Rādhā and Kṛṣṇa shone very beautifully in their midst."

doṇhāra rūpera phānde,   madana poriyā kānde
*   sudhākara kiraṇa lukāy*
doṇhāra mukhera vāṇī,   amiyā adhika śuni
*   sakhīgaṇa śravaṇa juṛāy*

"Cupid wept when he was trapped in the noose of Their lustrous forms and the moon hid his rays out of embarrassment. The words emanating from Their mouths sounded sweeter than nectar and soothed the ears of the *sakhīs*."

doṇhāra mādhurī guṇe,   ulasita sakhīgaṇe
*   nānā phule doṇhāre sājāy*
sugandhi candana diyā,   karpūra tāmbūla loiyā,
*   viśākhikā doṇhāre jogāy*

"The *sakhīs* were delighted by the attributes of Their sweetness and decorated Them with different flowers. Viśākhikā offered Them fragrant sandalwood pulp and camphor-laced betelleaves."

lalitā iṇgita pāiyā,   narmadā āilā loiyā,
*   vini sute gāṇthi phula hār*

deyolo doṇhāra gale, hiyāra upore dole,
dekhi āṅkhi śītala sabār

"Receiving Lalitā's beckoning, Narmadā came and brought stringless flower-garlands, hanging them around Their necks so that they dangled on Their chests. The eyes of everyone who saw this were soothed."

śekhara madhura kori, kohe kothā dhīri dhīri,
kānana śobhana dekhibāre
śuniyā catura kān, mone kori anumān,
uṭhilā dhanira dhari kore

"Rāya Śekhara gently speaks some sweet words — "Come and behold the beauty of the forest!" Hearing this, clever Kṛṣṇa thought to Himself and got up, holding Dhanī Rāi's hand." (110)

❀

vana bhramaāa
kedāra — tāla lophā

vinodinī vinoda nāgara kān;
sakhīgaṇa saṅge raṅge korolo payān
duhuṅ kāndhe duhu bhuja śobhiyāche bhālo;
duhuṅ rūpe daśa diśa koriyāche ālo

"Vinodinī (delightful Rādhā) and Vinoda Nāgara Kān (delightful hero Kṛṣṇa) thus set out in great bliss, accompanied by Their girlfriends. Their arms nicely beautified Each other's shoulders and Their forms illuminated the ten directions."

navīna yauvanī sab cole dui pāśe;
banera mādhurī dekhi hāsa parihāse

jāti jūthi mallikā mālatī nāgeśvara;
kadamba bokul dekhi campaka manohara
tamāla mādhavī bana ati gāḍhatara;
aśoka kiṁśuka donā dekhite sundara

"**Kṛṣṇa was thus flanked by young girls, beholding the sweetness of the forest and cracking jokes. They saw how beautiful the dense forest was with enchanting Jāti-, Yūthi-, Mallikā-, Nāgeśvara-, Kadamba-, Bakula-, Campaka-, Tamāla-, Mādhavī-, Aśoka- and Kiṁśuka-flowers.**"

vṛndāvane phala phule āche to bhoriyā;
mādhava mādhavī bhrame sakhīgaṇa loiyā
phula vana śobhā doṇhe dekhi anukhan;
phala vana dekhibāre korilā gaman

"**Vṛndāvana's forest is filled with fruits and flowers, and Mādhava and Mādhavī (Rādhā) took Their girlfriends on a tour of the woods. They constantly beheld the beauty of the flower forest, and then they went to admire the orchard.**"

ām jām bilva pilu guvāk nārikel;
bādām choharā nembu kapittha sakal
kamlā piyalā āra panasa kharjur;
drākhā darimba āmrātaka sumadhur
tāla kūla kalā ādi joteko kānan;
dekhi praphullita duhuṇ koroye bhraman
jantra-śālāte gelā nāgarī nāgara;
se beli vividha jantra jogāy śekhara

"**With minds blossoming of bliss they wandered through orchards of mango, Jambu (blackberries), Bilva,**"

Pilu, betel, coconut, peanut, date, lemon, Kapittha (shelled fruits), oranges, Piyalā-nuts, jackfruits, dates, grapes, pomegranates, very sweet hog plum, palm, berries and bananas. Then Nāgarī Rādhā and Nāgara Kṛṣṇa went to the Yantra-śālā (storehouse of musical instruments) where Rāya śekhara served Them by handing Them different instruments." (111)

saṅgīta rāsa
vihāga — tāla eka tālā

nīraja nayanī loilo vīṇa
sakala guṇaka ati pravīna
madhura madhura bāota tāla
madana mohana mohinī

"Lotus-eyed Rādhikā took the Vīṇā, and being very expert in all arts, began to play ever-so-sweet songs, enchanting the enchanter of Cupid!"

jhaṅkṛta jhaṅkṛta jhanana jhaṅka
colato aṅgulī lola taraṅga
kuṭila nayane koroto bhaṅga
aṅga bhaṅgī śohinī

"Her fingers made restless waves as they moved over the strings and She plays the śohinī (mode) with crooked eyes. How beautiful were Her bodily gestures!"

lalitā lalita dharata tāla
mohita mana mohana lāla
kohotahi ati bhāli bhāla
rādhikā guṇa śālinī

"Lovely Lalitā gave the rhythm, and mind-enchanting Kṛṣṇa was captivated and said: "Well done, well done!" Rādhikā is a reservoir of attributes!"

taruṇīgaṇa ekaho bheli,
sakala yantra korolo meli
muralī khuralī deota kāna
gamaki rāga mālinī

"The young girls joined together to play all musical instruments in harmony while Kṛṣṇa played His flute, in a modulating *mālinī rāga*."

matta kokila pañcama sura,
alikula tahi ati madhura,
muralī dhvani ghana garajani,
nācata mayūra mātiyā

"Intoxicated cuckoos sang in the fifth note the bumblebees sang sweetly with very nice voices, and as the flute resounded deeply, the peacocks danced like mad."

vṛndāvana sukhada dhāma,
tahi viharai rasika śyāma
tàruṇī gaṇa vimala vadana,
gāoto koto bhātiyā

"Vṛndāvana is a delightful abode and it is here that *rasika* śyāma enjoys Himself and the spotless-faced young girls sing to their hearts' content."

phuli anilo bahoi dhīra,
phuli coloi yamunā tīra
phuli kānana phuli madana
phuli boyonī śohinī

"The blossoming (joyful) breeze blew slowly, Yamunā joyfully flowed along its banks, the forests of Vraja blossomed of joy, Cupid blossomed of joy and the face of śohinī (beautiful and delightful Rāi) also blossomed."

lalitā kohoto madhura vāta
kānu nācata rāi sātha
aṅga bhaṅga sarasa raṅga
kohoto śekhara mohinī

"Lalitā spoke sweet words while Kānu danced with Rāi, moving His limbs in a very playful and succulent way. Thus Rāya śekhara narrates this story." (112)

Nṛtya Rāsa
belāvalī

nācata naṭavara kān;
rasavatī puna puna herai boyān
bājato koto koto jantra rasāl;
gāoto sahacari deoto tāl
caudige beṛhalo naṭinī samāj;
mājhe śobhato tahi naṭavara rāj
naṭa naṭinīgaṇa bhelo eka saṅga;
calato citra gati aṅga vibhaṅga
kore koro joṛi bhori nāce bālā;
madana gāṇthalo janu cāṇḍaki mālā

"Kṛṣṇa, the best of dancers, danced along, looking at the face of Rasavatī again and again. So many succulent instruments were played and so many girlfriends were giving the rhythm. Female dancers were dancing in a circle and the king of greatest dancers, śrī Kṛṣṇa, shone beautifully in the middle. The male dancer met with the female dancers and moved along, making the most wonderful bodily gestures. The girls danced hand in hand, as if Cupid had strung a garland of moons together."

> *padatala tāla dharaṇi para dhāri;*
> *nācato raṅgiṇī saṅge murāri*
> *heri lalitā sakhī leyali ḍampha;*
> *vikaṭa tāla taba koroli ārambha*
> *hāsi kamalamukhī kohe śuno kān;*
> *iha para padagati koroho suṭhān*
> *māti madana made madana gopāl;*
> *vikaṭa tāla para nācata rasāl*
> *rījhi deyoli dhanī motima māl*
> *sukha bhore śekhara kohe bhāli bhāli*

"According to the rhythm they kept their foot soles on the ground— thus Raṅgiāī Rāi danced with Murāri. Seeing this, Lalitā-*sakhī* took the ḍampha-drum and began a frantic rhythm. Lotus-faced Rāi smiled and said: "Listen, O Kṛṣṇa! Do some more of those wonderful dancing steps!" Madana Gopāla had became mad with lust and He began a frantic and succulent dance. Dhanī Rāi rewarded Him with Her pearl necklace and Rāya śekhara happily says: "Well done, well done!" (113)

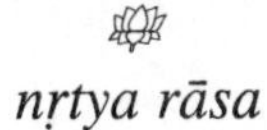

nṛtya rāsa

> *tattā thai thai bāoye mṛdaṅga;*
> *nācata vidhu mukhi aṅga vibhaṅga*
> *suviṣama tāla kānu jab delo*
> *taba lalitā sakhī haraṣita bhelo*

kānu kohe sundari koro avadhān;
iha para padagati koroho sandhān
raṅginī sahacari bāoto bhālo;
kānu deoto kore suviṣama tāl

"The *mṛdaṅga*-drums played *tattā thai thai* and Vidhumukhī (moon-faced Rāi) danced, making all kinds of physical gestures. When Kṛṣṇa made a very difficult rhythm Lalitā-*sakhī* became very happy. Kṛṣṇa said: "Sundari, watch this! Try to find a foot-step that is greater than this one! Playful Raṅgiāī Rāi and Her girlfriends said: "Very well" and Kṛṣṇa gave a very difficult rhythm.""

nācato suvadani kotohu suchanda;
heri camakita sab sahacarivṛnda
koi koho dhani dhani koi jayakāra;
kānu deolo taba nija guñjā hāra
kaṇṭhe deyolo dhani ura pora lāgo;
koho śekhara soi nava anurāga

"Suvadanī (fair-faced Rāi) then danced so beautifully, seeing which all the *sakhīs* were astonished. Some said: "Blessed, blessed You are!" while others exclaimed: "All glories to You!" Kṛṣṇa then rewarded Her by giving Her His own string of *guñjā*-berries. When He hung it around Dhani's neck it shone on Her breasts. Rāya śekhara says: "Such are the ways of young love!" (114)

rati vaicitrya
baḍārī rāga

madane vedana pāiyā madana gopāl;
dhorolo dhanīra kore nāhiko sambhāl

uca kuca kolose lālasa bhoi gelo;
saghane jaghana kāṁpe unamata bhelo
sakhīgaṇa toikhona koilo anumāna;
cololo campaka vana loi rāi kān

"Madana Gopāla became tormented by Cupid and He held Dhani's hand without obstruction. He became lusty after Her raised, jug-like breasts and began to shiver vehemently as if He were mad. The *sakhīs* then thought: 'Let's take Rāi-Kān to the forest of Campaka-vines."

praphulla kānana tāhe maṇimoya ghar;
sukhada śejera mājhe bosilā nāgar
sakhī pāśe bosi hāse rāi sudhāmukhī;
nāgare kātara dekhi hāse sab sakhī
sveda jale bhorolo sakala kalevare;
śekhara ghucāya śrama nānā upacāre

"On a delightful bed in a jewelled cottage within this blossoming garden, Nāgara sat down and smiling Rāi Sudhāmukhī (nectar-faced Rādhā) sat with Him, flanked by Her girlfriends. When they saw how anxious Nāgara was, they smiled. His whole body was studded with sweat drops, but Rāya śekhara removed this sign of fatigue with different paraphernalia of service. (115)

sakhī śikṣā
rāgiāī dhānaśī

ei dhani paduminī śuno majhu bāt;
aichana mīlabi nāyara sāth
jatane basana aṅge rākhobi goi;
rohobi lājāi janu bāta nā hoi

avanata boyāne rohobi kṣiti heri;
khene ādha nayane cāhobi beriberi
khene kuca-yuga cīra korobi udās;
khene khene chorobi dīgha niśvās

"O Lotus-like fortunate girl! Hear My words! This is how You meet with Your hero. Carefully conceal Your body with Your cloth. Remain shy and silent. Look at the ground with lowered head. Look again and again with half opened eyes at one time, and at another time pull Your veil nonchalantly over Your breasts, and at yet another time breathe out deeply."

khene khene nivi bandha bāndhobi jhāri;
nirakhi lubadha janu hoyoto murāri
jabahu jatana tohe korobohu nāho;
niraba nā bolabi vacana niravāho
surata piyāse piyā dharabahu hāth;
anumati nā deobi dhulāyabi māth
kore korobo jab rasika sujān;
parihāra māgabi pālaṭi boyān

"Sometimes bind Your girdle up tightly, so that Murāri will get lusty when He sees it. When Your hero comes and approaches You, then don't stay silent but stop Him with Your words. When Your beloved, who is thirsty for eros, holds Your hand, then don't grant Him permission, but shake Your head. When Rasika Sujān Kṛṣṇa takes You on His lap then turn Your face away and ask Him to let go."

jab tohe anumati cāhabo kān;
lahu lahu bolabi amiyā samān
cumbana beri korobi mukha baṅkā;

surati samaya janu pāabi śaṅkā
koho kavi śekhara colu sukumārī;
tuyā lāgi ākula bhelo murāri

"When Kṛṣṇa seeks Your permission then speak to Him with a soft, ambrosial voice. When He wants to kiss You, then turn away Your face and when the time for love-making is there, then show fear." Kavi śekhara says: "Go, Sukumāri (tender Rādhā)! Murāri is very eager for You!" (116)

❁

āligaāera cāturī

sakhīgaṇa tokhoni,   bodhi kula kāminī
leyoto piyā kara pāśa
vipine hariṇī janu,   vyādha hi bāndholo
aichana tejoto śvāsa

"As Her girlfriends thus addressed Kula Kāminī Rāi they took Her to Her beloved, who was panting like a doe that was caught by a hunter."

kore ṭheli ṭheli bāli,   ālikula ānali
ṭhamaki ṭhamaki rohi jāy
pada nakhe dharaṇī,   vidārai kāminī
camaki camaki ghana cāy

"Kicking around the sand, the girls brought Her over. She showed different bodily gestures, renting the soil with Her foot nails and staring around in astonishment."

kaṭi kiṅkinī dhani,   dṛḍha kori bāndhai
puna puna nūpura bājāy

tāhi chale bhuja mūla,　　vasana udāsalo
pi-ā hi-e madana jāgāy

"Dhani firmly bound Her belt of bells around Her waist and Her anklebells jingled again and again. On top of that She showed Her armpits through Her garments and thus Cupid awoke in Kṛṣṇa's heart."

āra nayana kori,　　hari mukha heroi
vacana racai ati mīṭh
nāhoko vacana;　　śravaṇe nāhi śunoi
lāgi roholo āli pīṭh

"With half-closed eyes She looked at Hari's face and spoke very sweet words. Her ears did not hear Kṛṣṇa's words, as She and Her *sakhīs* stood with their backs towards Him."

kānu manohāriṇī,　　saha nava raṇgiṇī,
bhaṇginī koru koto chanda
koho kavi śekhara,　　śuno vara nāgara,
nava rasa pāna makaranda

"How many gestures this girl, who steals Kṛṣṇa's mind, made, along with Her young playful confidantes! Kavi Śekhara says: "Listen, O best of amorous heroes! Drink the nectar of fresh flavours!"" (117)

❀

nāyaka śikṣā

e hari! nāyarī navīnā bālā; kāminī mānāyobi koriyā chalā
jokhon je mukhe dāṛāye rāi; korobi minati sekhāne jāi
binoya vebhāre ānobi pāś; madhura vacane deyobi hās
je bele sarasa dekhobi tāy; se bele paraśa korobi gāy

"O Hari! This heroine is a young girl, but You somehow consider Her a woman. Wherever Rāi is standing, go there in a humble way. Attract Her with this humble conduct, smile at Her and speak sweet words to Her. Whenever She looks at You in a *rasika* way, You can go and touch Her body."

tāhāte tāhāra dekhobi sukh; tabe se cumbana korobi mukh
se sab sakala sahilo jabe; pīna payodhara dharabi tabe
boyana cumbane ghucābi lāj; loiyā bosābi urubo mājh
nībi khosāyobi bhujera bole; hāsa parihāse korobi kole

"When You see that this makes Her happy, then You can proceed by kissing Her on the face. If She tolerates all this then You can grab Her big breasts and give up all shame by kissing Her on the mouth and seating Her on Your thighs. With the strength of Your arms You can open Her girdle and take Her on Your lap while laughing and joking."

madana āsana paraśa kori; rahobi bālāra boyāna heri
yadi vā jubatī muruchā jāy; deyobi candana korobi bāy
alape alape sādhabi sādha; navīna ālāpe nā koro bād
śekhara nāgare śikhāya hita; rasika janāra ei se rīta

"Touching Cupid's seat (Her buttocks), continue looking at this girl's face. If this young girl faints, then anoint Her body with sandalwood pulp. In this way You gradually achieve Your goal. Don't engage in any new talks." Rāya śekhara instructs Nāgara Kṛṣṇa for His own benefit— "such are the ways of *rasika* persons." (118)

🪷

saṅkṣipta sambhoga
vihagaḍā / vibhāṣa rāgiāī — tāla daśa kusi

hari kore hariṇī, nayanī taba sompiyā,
 sakhigaṇa colu ān ṭhāme
avasare dhani kore, dhari vara nāgara,
 minati koroye anupāme

"Fawn-eyed Rādhā held Hari's hand and came along, Her *sakhīs* walking on Her other side. The best of amorous heroes, Kṛṣṇa, held Dhani Rāi's hand in an incomparibly humble way."

 hariṇī nayanī dhani rāmā
kānuka sarasa, paraśa sambhāṣaṇe
 meṭa-u lājaki dhāmā

"Fawn-eyed Dhani Rāi's abode of bashfulness was destroyed when She heard Kṛṣṇa's succulent words and felt His succulent touch."

sukhaḍa śejopara, rāi loi nāgara,
 baiṭhali nava rati sādhe
prati aṅge cumbane, rasa anumodane,
 tharahari kāṁpaye rādhe

"Nāgarī Rāi took Her Nāgara on a delightful bed of love, accomplishing yet new desires for amorous love. Kissing Each of His limbs and relishing Their flavours, Rādhā shivered profusely."

madana siṁhāsane koroli ārohaṇa
 mohana rasika sujāna

bhoy pāi toṛala,   alape samādhalo,
rākhalo sakala samāna

"Mohana, the great *rasika*, then (also) mounted Cupid's throne. Her rebukes frightened Him, though, and He completed His actions quickly, keeping everything as it was."

koho kavi śekhara,   guruyā bhokha bhara,
koru jala thora āhāre
aichana duhu jana,   talapa hi punaḥ puna,
upajalo adhika vikāre

"Kavi Śekhara says: Becoming greatly hungry, They drank a little water. Thus these two lovers repeatedly experienced so many ever-increasing ecstatic transformations in bed." (119)

❀

saṅkīrāa sambhoga

puna hari nāgarī,   cumboi beri beri,
adhara sudhā koru pān
madana mahodadhi,   uchali uchali paṛu
ḍubalo nāgara kān

"Hari kissed His heroine again and again, drinking the nectar from Her lips. Thus the ocean of Cupid surged and immersed Nāgara Kān."

uca kuca kalasa,   paraśa kori nāgara,
bhāsoi yauvana bāne
nava rati sukhe,   dukha dhanī bhāvoi
nāho minati nāhi māne

"Nāgara Kṛṣṇa touched Her raised, jug-like breasts and floated on Her youthful beauty. He did not consider that Dhani would suffer during His new erotic happiness and ignored Her humble pleas."

kapaṭa roi dhani, piyā kara vāroi,
* kore kuca roholi jhāṁpāi*
vithāralo keśa, veśa nīvi bandhana,
* ura muri āsana chāpāi*

"Rāi Dhanī falsely cried and stopped Kṛṣṇa's hands, covering Her breasts with Her hands. She dropped Her long hairs over Her garments and the strings of Her girdle, and concealed Her private parts by contracting Her thighs."

vikaṭa kapaṭa dibo, kori nava nāgara
* nāgari kore bosāi*
ghana kuca mardane, dṛḍha parirambhaṇe
* kapaṭe murache dhani rāi*

"Our young hero used oaths, force and tricks to seat Nāgarī Rāi on Her lap. He massaged Her big breasts and tightly embraced Her, so Dhani Rāi pretended to faint."

surati samara rase, kānu mana mātalo,
* kamalini kātara bālā*
sab aṅga śithila, sveda jale tītalo
* maradita campaka mālā*

"Kṛṣṇa's mind became heated in the flavours of the erotic battle and lotus-like Rāi got all agitated also. All Her limbs slackened and sweatdrops dripped from Her person, making Her resemble a crushed garland of golden Campaka-flowers (or: Her garland of Campaka flowers was crushed).”

> *dhani heri nāgara, poṛolohi phāmpar*
>   *choṛalo keli vilāsa*
> *koho kavi śekhara, kānu bhelo kātara,*
>   *cīrahi koroto bātās*

“When Nāgara Kṛṣṇa saw Dhani Rāi He lost His mind and gave up His playful games. Kavi śekhara says: “Kṛṣṇa became overwhelmed, so I fanned Him with my cloth.” (120)

rāginī — dhānaśī

> *cīra pavane dhani śītala bhelo;*
> *charama gharama saba dūrahi gelo*
> *baiṭhalo duhuṅ jab śejako māho;*
> *taba anumānalo rasika sunāho*
> *rāiko iha sab kapaṭa tarāsa;*
> *bujhiyā rasika vara lahu lahu hāsa*
> *tahi puna cumbai rāi-boyān;*
> *duhuṅ jana marame hānalo pāñca bāṇa*
> *puna bilasaye duhuṅ heraite dhanda;*
> *koho kavi śekhara hi parabandha*

“Being thus fanned by a garment, Dhanī cooled off and the sweatdrops caused by Their erotic climax was removed. They both sat up on the bed and Rasika Nāgara thought to Himself: ‘All this is Rāi’s false fear.’ Understanding this, that greatest of *rasikas* laughed softly to Himself and kissed Rāi’s face again. Thus Both Their hearts were (again) pierced by Cupid. Kavi śekhara thus describes how they re-started Their bewildering loving pastimes. (121)

sampanna sambhoga
rāga kedāra

sukhamaya vṛndāvane sukhamaya śyām;
sukhamayī rādhikā tahi anupām
duhuṇ mili rasa keli koru ānande;
duhuṇ adharāmṛte bhoru mukha cande
duhuṇ tanu pulakita duhuṇ mana bhor;
vinodinī rādhā vinodiyā kor
duhuṇ keli paṇḍita rūpe guṇe sam;
vilāsa vibhramā rase keho nohe kom
surati mūrati dohe koru parakāś;
rati pati antare lāgalo tarās

"**Vṛndāvana is blissful, śyāma is blissful and śrī Rādhikā is incomparibly blissful. The *rasika* pastimes They perform together are so blissful and Their moon-like faces are filled with the nectar of Their lips. Their bodies are studded with goosepimples and Their minds are absorbed (in love-mellows). Vinodinī Rādhā sits on Vinodī Kṛṣṇa's lap. They are both expert in love-play and They are equally beautiful and qualified. They are also unable to defeat Each other in *vilāsa vibhrama rasa* (the flavours of bewildering love-sports). They both reveal the embodiment of eros, causing anxiety to the heart of the Lord of Rati (Cupid)."**

adabhuta ratiraṇa dūre rohu lāj;
nūpura runu runu kiṇkiṇī bāj

akhaṇḍa vilāsa rasa nāhi bhelo vād;
duhuṇ mili pūralo janamaka sādh
eka tanu eka mana ekoi parāṇ;
duhuṇ aṅga eka koilo vidhi niramāṇ
śrama jale bhīgalo duhu jana gāy;
duhuṇ rati sāyare ora nāhi pāy
duhuṇ dohā cumboi samādhai keli
; duhuṇ jana sevane śekhara geli

"Due to Their amazing erotic fight Their shame had fled far away. Their waistbells and anklebells jingled and there was no end or obstruction to the flavours of Their loving pastime. By thus uniting with Each other They fulfilled the wish of a lifetime. The Creator had made Their bodies, minds and life airs as one. Their bodies were moistened by drops of perspiration and Neither of Them could find the end to Their ocean of erotic bliss. They completed Their love game by kissing Each other and then Rāy śekhara went in to serve Them both." (122)

viparīta śṛṅgāra
vihagaḍā

kāminī baiṭhali kānuka saṅga; kṣaṇe kṣaṇe upajaye nava
nava raṅga
nāyari cumbai nāho vayāṇ; so sukha sāyare bhāsolo kān
dhani mana manamathe unamata bhelā;
nāgara upara payodhara delā
kāmini karatahi puruṣa ācārā;
jiu loi bhāgoi lāj becārā
ulaṭalo loṭana uru para caraṇā;
nikasolo śramajala aparūpa karaṇā

"Kāminī Rādhā sat with Kṛṣṇa, making new fun at every moment. Nāgarī Rāi kissed Nāgara Kṛṣṇa's face, making Him float in an ocean of bliss. Dhani's mind was also maddened by Cupid and She placed Her breasts on Nāgara's chest. Kāminī Rāi thus behaved like a man (taking the upper position). Bashfulness was assaulted and fled in a helpless way. In this reversed position She placed Her lotus feet on Kṛṣṇa's thighs and this wonderful conduct caused sweat drops to emanate from Her pores."

nāsā khagapati śvāsa hilori;
jalada upore dole vinoda vijori
rati ati viparīta vilasai kāminī
mana sidhi sādhai jāgai jāminī
duhu mana mānasa pūraṇa bheli;
haraṣi saroja mukhi samādhalo keli
vilāse alasa bhelo duhu jana gāy;
śramajala dūra koru śekhara rāy

"Their nostrils breathed out waves of air like Garuḍa. A blissful lightning (Rādhā) swayed on top of a cloud (Kṛṣṇa). Thus Kāminī Rādhā enjoyed reverse pastimes and stayed up the whole night, fulfilling Her heart's wishes. Their minds were fulfilled, so blissfully Saroja Mukhī (lotus-faced Rādhā) ended the game of love. Their bodies had become tired of love-making and so Rāya Śekhara helps in removing Their perspiration (by fanning Them)." (123)

rasollāsa

kānu kohe śaśimukhi koro avadhāno;
tuhuṇ rati raṇa vīra ab hām jāno

tuyā ṭhām ṭhamake camaka bhelo kām;
bhāgi roholo dūre gaṇi pariṇām
tuhuṇ dhani koroli joichana keli;
hām nāhi jāniye aichana meli
ab hām guru kori mānaluṇ toy;
adabhuta rati rīti śikhāyali moy

"Kṛṣṇa said: "Listen carefully, O moon-faced girl! Now I understand that You are a heroine in the battle of eros! Your gestures astonished Cupid and caused him to flee and offer his obeisances from a distance. O fortunate girl! I have never seen anyone playing the game of love the way You did when You united with Me. Now I consider You My Guru— You tought Me all these amazing arts of love!"

adhare daśana cihna deyoli haṭhinī;
hṛdoya vidāralo tuyā kuca kaṭhinī
nakhare vidārolo sab tanu mor;
tileka karuṇā dhani nā rohu tor
koho kavi śekhara śuno vara kān;
ājanama guru guṇa korobi dheyān

"You forcibly make teeth-marks on My lips and Your hard breasts break My heart (they rent My chest apart). Your nails have torn up My whole body— O fortunate girl, You don't have even the slightest compassion!" Kavi śekhara says: "Listen, O excellent Kṛṣṇa! You should meditate on the attributes of Your Guru (Rādhā) for the rest of Your life!" (124)

sakhīgaāer vākye śrī kṛṣṇa kartṛk śrī rādhār veśa racanā

sakhīgaṇa kohe śuno nāgara kān;
viracaho rāiko veśa banān

sīnthi racana kori deho sindur;
cibukahi mṛgamada racaho madhur
nayanahi añjana yāvaka pāy;
pīna payodhara citraho tāya
aichana vacana tab śunaite pāy;
śekhara veśa sājalo dhāi

The *sakhīs* said: Listen O lover Kāna! Make a dress for Rāi. Place *sindūra* in Her part, place a sweet muskdrop on Her chin, put collyrium around Her eyes, lac on Her feet and pictures on Her big breasts." Hearing such words, śekhara runs to make such a dress. (125)

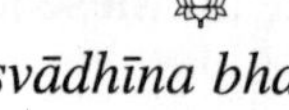

svādhīna bhartṛkā
mallāra rāga

aparūpa rādhā mādhava nehā
rasavatī veśa,   bonāite rasamaya,
avaśa bhoi gelo dehā

"How wonderful is Rādhā-Mādhava's love! Rasamaya śyāma's body was overwhelmed by ecstasy as He made a dress for Rasavatī Rāi."

punahun sambhāri,   nāgarī sājāite
ghana ghana kara koru kampa
kuca yuga paraśe,   avaśalo tanu mana,
lore nayana rahu jhampa

"Again Kṛṣṇa engaged Himself in decorating Nāgari Rāi, while His hands shook vehemently. His body and mind were overwhelmed as He touched Her breasts and tears squirted out from His eyes."

koto anubandha, koroto nava nāgara,
  nāgarī kore bosāi
caraṇa kamala pora, nūpura porāite,
  gole gajamoti khosāi

"How humbly our young amorous hero requested His heroine to be seated! As He hung anklebells above Her lotus feet a pearl necklace fell from His neck."

bharame bhorolo tanu, camaki roholo kānu,
  vinodinī vadana nehāri·
jubati jatana kori, sājāyalo sahacarī
  śekhara kohe bolihāri

"Kṛṣṇa became so astonished when He gazed at Vinodinī Rāi's face that His body became filled with bewilderment. Thus Yuvatī Rādhā's maidservants had to take over Her dressing, to which Rāya Śekhara says: "Bravo!" (126)

❁

madana madālasa
rāgiāī belāvalī — tāla eka tālā

ālase ākula bhelo rasavatī rāi;
madana madālase śutali jāi
kānu śayana koru kāminī kor;
cāṇda āgori janu raholo cakor
duhu śire duhu bhuje boyāne boyān;
ūru ūru lapaṭalo nayāne nayān
ghūmi roholo tahi kiśorī kiśor;
keśa praveśa nāhi tanu tanu joṛ
sakhīgaṇa nija nija kuñje payān;
nibhṛta niketane korolo śayān
sveda bindu dekhi duhu jana gāy;
śekhara korotohi cāmara bāy

"Rasavatī Rāi became overwhelmed by erotic fatigue and reclined on the bed; Kṛṣṇa reclined on Her lap, relishing Her as the Cakora bird relishes the moonlight. They embraced Each other and Their faces, thighs and eyes also met. Thus Kiśorī and Kiśora fell asleep, so tightly embracing Each other that not even a hair could be stuck in between Their bodies. The *sakhīs* then all retired to their individual *kuñjas* and went to sleep in solitude. Rāya śekhara sees sweatdrops on Their bodies and starts to fan Them with a yaktail fan." (127)

❁

nidrālasa
rāginī rāma kelī — tāla eka tālā

alasahi nāgarī, kusuma śeja pori,
* śutali nāgarakor*
* kiye rati pati, tūṇ bhelo bāṇ śūn,*
* kiye bihi korolo vibhor*

"Exhausted, Nāgarī Rāi reclined on the chest of Her Nāgara on the bed of flowers. Has Ratipati (Cupid) fired all the arrows from his quiver, or has Fate become completely overwhelmed?"

dekho duhuṇ nindaka raṇga
kanaka latāye, tamāle janu beṛhalo
* cāṇda suruja ek saṇga*

"Behold Their blissful pastime of sleep! They resembled a golden vine entwining a Tamāla-tree or the moon and the sun in one place."

bayānahi bayān, bhujahi bhuja bandhana,
* caraṇa hi caraṇa veyāpi*

taṛita hi jaṛita,   jaiche nava jaladhara,
     śaśī rohu timira hi jhāpi

"**They kept Their faces near Each other, wrapped Their arms around Each other and kept Their feet intertwined also. Thus They resembled a fresh monsoon cloud entwined by a lightning strike, or a moon shining in the dark night.**"

kanaka meru juga,   nīla jaladhi jale,
     ḍubalo heno anumāni
aichana aparupa,   ko koru anubhava,
     koho kavi śekhara jāni

"**I think Rādhikā's breasts resemble two golden mountains drowning in a blue ocean (Kṛṣṇa's chest). Who can experience these things in such a wonderful way? Kavi Śekhara knows it, for he describes it.**" (128)

Thus ends Rāya Śekhara's Aṣṭakāla līlā Padāvalī.